Twayne's United States Authors Series

EDITOR OF THIS VOLUME

Kenneth Eble
University of Utah

Lincoln Steffens

TUSAS 320

Lincoln Steffens

LINCOLN STEFFENS

By PATRICK F. PALERMO

University of Dayton

TWAYNE PUBLISHERS

A DIVISION OF G. K. HALL & CO., BOSTON

Published in 1978 by Twayne Publishers,
A Division of G. K. Hall & Co.
All Rights Reserved

Printed on permanent/durable acid-free paper and bound
in the United States of America

First Printing

Library of Congress Cataloging in Publication Data

Palermo, Patrick F
Lincoln Steffens.

(Twayne's United States authors series ; TUSAS 320)
Bibliography: p. 141 - 45
Includes index.
1. Steffens, Joseph Lincoln, 1866 - 1936.
2. Journalists—United States—Biography.
PN4874.S68P34   070.4'092'4 [B]   78-17800
ISBN 0-8057-7253-7

To Jeanne and Patrick

Contents

About the Author

Born in the Bronx and raised in Watertown, New York, Professor Palermo received his A.B. Phi Beta Kappa from Fordham College. In 1973, he completed his Ph.D. at the State University of New York at Stony Brook. Greatly interested in the relationship between community and politics, he has presented papers on that subject to such groups as the Organization of American Historians. Professor Palermo has published articles in various scholarly journals, including *Capitol Studies*. Among the grants and fellowships awarded him was a two year curriculum grant from the National Endowment for the Humanities. Presently, he is an Assistant Professor of American history at the University of Dayton and the director of the University's Honors Program.

Preface

Lincoln Steffens, noted journalist, muckracker, and social critic, was an important figure during one of the pivotal periods of our history. His life and work exemplify the efforts of nineteenth century America to come to grips with twentieth century realities. His youth reflected the values and experience of semifrontier, entrepreneurial, small town California. His early career as a journalist found him confronting the problems and possibilities of urban, industrial society. His later years as a free-lance writer saw him struggling with a world gone mad with war, revolution, and depression. The very fact that he witnessed and participated in these momentous times makes his life worth knowing and his articles, essays, short stories, and books well worth reading. Yet, his life, however fascinating, should not overshadow the importance of understanding how Steffens reported the news and saw himself in the world. Consequently, this is a critical-analytical study of Lincoln Steffens' writings and not a biography.

By examining his work critically, I think that it is possible to appreciate his classic American approach to understanding man and society, his brilliance as an investigative reporter, and his both ordinary and extraordinary political beliefs. Like so many of his contemporaries, Steffens believed that direct, individual experience was the basis for the best and most trustworthy knowledge. This manner of learning has been called pragmatism by American intellectuals and practicality by businessmen. For American authors, this continual demand for personal experience has been a dynamic source of their creativity. Steffens shared with millions of American citizens the belief that experience shaped a man's character and provided him with the essential knowledge for a satisfying, useful life. In this sense, the frontier has always been a metaphor for the willingness of Americans to confront new experiences with optimism. From his first newspaper article to his *Autobiography*, Steffens' writing reflected this exuberance for the active life.

My contention is that this obsession with experience combined with a peculiarly American innocence to make Steffens a great and popular journalist. For most of his long career, he maintained a readiness to look at man, institutions, and movements without prejudice. His newspaper and magazine pieces contain the excitement of discovery. He always wanted to be at the center of the action. Whether it be in New York in the 1890s or in Russia after the revolution, he needed to understand the story and to share that knowledge with his readers. Steffens loved to play detective, ferreting out the truth under the hypocrisy that he was sure covered so many of man's misdeeds. In this role, he became the nation's foremost muckraker with his investigations of American cities. Despite the fame and reputation he gained with *The Shame of the Cities,* Steffens never lost his appreciation for news. He continued to approach each new assignment with some awe and much anticipation.

Throughout his career, Steffens displayed the attitude of the pilgrim in search of understanding. When faced with an unfamiliar situation, he deferred to those who were deeply involved in the particular experience. His success as an interviewer was at least partly due to his obvious readiness to learn from his subjects. He reserved his greatest admiration for those who grasped the essence of the experience and then took command of their environment. As a result, his heroes ranged from ward heelers to reform mayors and, finally, to Russian revolutionaries. This, I believe, was his blind spot as a reporter and social critic. Steffens thought that powerful men who had steeped themselves in their social milieu would, if given the opportunity, do what was best for themselves and their fellow man. This conviction served as a basis for much of his political philosophy.

Steffens was an intensely political journalist who began his career as a typical American reformer and ended it as a disillusioned liberal defending communism. His writings are a veritable history of the rise and fall of reform consciousness in the first decades of this century. Like so many progressives, Steffens had a deep-seated faith in progress that was based on his belief that man is essentially good. He was as sure as any progressive that once the people recognized the evils of society, they would support reform. The equation was simple. Corruption flourished in an atmosphere of ignorance and deception. When informed of the true conditions of their cities and states by the muckrakers, the aroused citizenry would rise up and defeat their enemies at the polls. During twenty years of reform, Steffens remained convinced that the application of good will and intelligence to social problems was the essence of progress. Although he eventually rejected this approach to politics and social change as being too simplistic, Steffens never found an adequate substitute.

With the failure of Woodrow Wilson at the Paris Peace Conference and the victory of the Bolsheviks in Russia, Steffens saw the tide of history turn against liberalism. After much soul searching, he denounced reform and embraced the idea of revolution. Despite his defense of the Communist experiment in Russia, the aging journalist could not escape looking at the twentieth century from a nineteenth century perspective. Like Moses in his revolutionary parable, *Moses In Red*, Steffens could not cross over into the promised land of the revolutionaries. Since he was excluded from the future, he settled for some understanding of his life. *The Autobiography* is the tale of a man measuring himself as a moral agent in the world. It is a story as old as America.

The following people have contributed much to the merits of this book and nothing to its failings. Rocco Donatelli was instrumental in my undertaking this study. The chairman of my department, Leroy Eid, supported my research and writing with generous grants of time and the use of the department's staff and resources. In this regard, I would like to thank Lois Howe for typing the manuscript with care and precision. Many people read and criticized my work. Among my colleagues who took time to review the manuscript were John McClymer, Alfred Bannan, and Johannah Sherrer. Robert Marcus was an exacting critic who, although I may not have achieved it, pointed the way to excellence. Roberta Alexander watched over the manuscript as if it were her own. Her encouragement always sent me back to work with renewed enthusiasm. Raymond Cunningham put his erudition and superb critical abilities at my service. Always generous with his time and praise, he gently guided me to correct my stylistic and analytic errors.

I am grateful to the University of Dayton for a research grant that made possible much of the writing of this book.

Chronology

1866   April 6: Joseph Lincoln Steffens born in San Francisco. From the first, he is called by his middle name.
1870   Family moves to Sacramento, where Steffens grows up.
1881   Joseph Steffens sends his son to military school in San Mateo to learn discipline.
1885   Steffens enrolls at the University of California at Berkeley.
1889   Graduates from Berkeley near bottom of his class. Enters the University of Berlin for graduate studies in experimental psychology and ethics.
1890   Attends universities at Heidelberg and Leipzig. Meets Josephine Bontecou in Paris.
1891   Studies in Paris; marries Josephine.
1892   Returns to the United States and his father cuts off financial support. Becomes reporter for *New York Evening Post*.
1893   Covers Wall Street and becomes *Post* reporter at police headquarters.
1894   Helps the Reverend Parkhurst throw Tammany Hall out of office in New York.
1895   Meets Theodore Roosevelt.
1897   Leaves the *Evening Post* to become city editor for the *New York Commercial Advertiser*.
1901   Accepts position of managing editor with *McClure's Magazine*.
1902   The first article about corruption in St. Louis appears in *McClure's*.
1903   The January issue of *McClure's* has articles by Ida Tarbell, Ray Stannard Baker, and Steffens. This signals the beginning of modern muckraking.
1904   *The Shame of the Cities* is published. Steffens' series, "Enemies of the People," begins in *McClure's*.
1906   *The Struggle for Self-Government* is published. Steffens leaves *McClure's* to become part owner of *American Magazine*.
1907   After a dispute over editorial policy, Steffens sells his share of *American Magazine*.

1908   A. E. Filene hires Steffens to help reform Boston.

1909   *Upbuilders* is published.

1910   Walter Lippmann works with Steffens on government and business corruption.

1911   Josephine dies. Steffens moves to Greenwich Village, where he becomes John Reed's mentor and a regular participant at Mabel Dodge's salon. Steffens arbitrates the McNamara case in Los Angeles.

1914   Goes to Mexico to observe that nation's revolution.

1917   Visits Russia for the first time soon after the overthrow of the czar.

1918   Tours the United States, trying to prepare the nation for peace.

1919   Goes to Russia as a member of Bullitt Mission. Meets Ella Winter in Paris.

1920   Is nearly hounded out of the United States for defending the Russian Revolution. Moves to Europe.

1923   Visits Russia for third and final time.

1924   Marries Ella Winter; Peter, Steffens' only child, is born.

1926   *Moses In Red* is published.

1927   Homesick, Steffens returns to the United States and settles in Carmel, California.

1931   *The Autobiography of Lincoln Steffens* is published.

1933   After suffering a stroke while on a lecture tour, Steffens is a semi-invalid.

1936   *Lincoln Steffens Speaking* is published. Steffens dies on August 9.

CHAPTER 1

Hustling in New York

IN October 1892, Lincoln Steffens arrived in New York. Behind him was a happy childhood in California, a mediocre college career at Berkeley, and three restless years of postgraduate education in Europe spent seeking a "scientific basis" for ethics. With him was his bride, Josephine Bontecou, and her mother, Susan. Waiting for Steffens was a letter from his father containing one hundred dollars and the advice that his son "stay in New York and hustle." Ahead of him was an unexpected career as one of the foremost American journalists of the twentieth century.[1]

Steffens was typical of his generation, which would create new fields, develop new professions, and build new institutions. Yet, like so many others, his background gave little or no inkling that he would be much different from his parents. Steffens belonged to the entrepreneurial middle class that was the backbone of national stability in the last century. His father was a successful businessman who migrated from the Middle West to build a substantial fortune in pioneer California. During his childhood, Steffens was the pride and joy of his entire family. His mother and three sisters showered him with affection as his father did with understanding. Until his return from Europe, his parents had satisfied almost his every whim and waited patiently for their son to take his proper place within genteel society. Despite all these advantages, Steffens was a discontented young man.

Yet, his dissatisfaction was not a sign of deep-seated alienation. He did not harbor any distaste for his parents, their values, or the West. Nevertheless, he was unwilling to accept their way of life as his own. Like a number of his contemporaries, his trip to Europe was an intermediary step toward personal independence. Steffens was not so much searching for an objective method for measuring human conduct at German and French universities as he was slowly preparing to strike out on his own. Upon returning to the United

15

States, he quickly began a career that would bring him much fame and some fortune. In this light, the letter he received from his father can be most instructive.

Reconstructed from his memory in *The Autobiography*, the letter was an ultimatum. His father had finally given up hope that his son would return to Sacramento and carry on his business interests. His son had done enough preparing for life; it was time to live it. Consequently, he was cutting his son off some three thousand miles from home. How perfect this was for the young Steffens. Relieved of all guilt, he could plunge into a career of his own making. What else could he do? His father had given him no choice in the matter. Steffens was not bitter but, in fact, appeared overjoyed by his predicament. He did not even tell his parents that he was recently married, perhaps fearful that such information would change their minds. No doubt there was more of Steffens than his father in this letter. Steffens might have it both ways; he could have his own life without a painful revolt against his family and their world.[2]

What was absent in Steffens was any profound tension with his own culture. His actions and writing displayed his ambiguous feelings toward the middle class and its values. He greatly respected his father but had no inclination to follow in his footsteps. Although he fondly remembered his childhood, he refused to accept the familial society of his parents. Despite four years at Berkeley and three more in European universities, he insisted that formal education was often worse than useless. Professing to despise the business world, his first impulse in New York was to look for commercial opportunity. His relationship with Josephine did not end in a brief bohemian affair on the Left Bank but in a perfectly conventional marriage. He loved the West, but settled on the other end of the American continent. In short, Steffens was no angry young man, and his rebellion was tentative at best.

Steffens well understood this and wrote about it in his semiautobiographical short story, "A Dismal Holiday." In this tale, written by Steffens at the turn of the century, the two protagonists are young Californians who are "discontented" with their school vacation plans. There is a strong hint of irony as the boys "grumble" about recreational opportunities that would be the envy of the average adolescent. Tired of hunting, fishing, riding, swimming, and canoeing, they decide to visit the largest ranch in the region and watch the cowboys work. The holiday that follows closely resembles one described by Steffens in his *Autobiography*. Riding

out from home, the two boys swim, catch a "bag full of fish," and
run down some rabbits. Arriving at the ranch in time for supper,
they share their catch with the cowboys, who regale the youngsters
with "wonderful stories." The scene is marred slightly by a ranch
hand from the East who is jealous of the joys of growing up in
California. Henry, one of the two boys, can not understand what
the young Easterner could possibly mean by his remarks. In a
postscript, Henry decides to go East to attend college. There he is
amazed to find his classmates dreaming of the West. This does not
deter Henry from his own goal; "he intended to stay east and he
did."[3]

On the surface, "A Dismal Holiday" provides no motivation for
the hero's desire to move East. The story lacks any real dramatic
tension, and Steffens, who obviously patterned Henry on himself,
fully realized it. Because the holiday is so idyllic, it is impossible to
believe that Steffens stayed East because of any substantial dissatisfaction with life in California. By denying that the decision was
based on any intrinsic alienation from his childhood in the West,
Steffens made his point. The only possible explanation for Henry's
move was the natural restlessness of youth. He went East, and his
counterparts moved in the opposite direction. Steffens' need to
leave California was based on the pull of the unknown, not dis-
pleasure with the known. The very finality of his protagonist's
pronouncement indicated the necessity of such a move. Unlike Nick
Carraway in *The Great Gatsby*, once Steffens decided to make his
own way in an unfamiliar world there was no turning back. There
must be some pain in giving up such an attractive environment as
California, but this was the price of personal freedom and opportunity.

Earlier, Steffens had written a short story, "Hon. Frank Ditson,"
that portrayed the fate of a young man who did not leave his home
in the West. The hero, a student at Berkeley, is a "powerfully built"
son of a prosperous rancher who is innocent of all urban "vices."
Like Steffens' own college experience, Ditson discovers the adventure of learning and meets a young woman, Mary Benson. Unlike
the author, Frank Ditson remains in California after graduation and
enters the "active life" of business. He slowly loses his innocence
and becomes a cynical practitioner of commercial and political
manipulation. After rejecting his girl for being too childish and unsophisticated, he eventually decides to marry her, realizing that her
father is a powerful politician who can help Ditson's career. The

story ends with Ditson proclaiming to the world that he would let
"nothing pure or good or sweet deter" him from success.[4]

Written by Steffens while he was still studying in Europe, the
story strongly suggests that he had already made up his mind not to
return to California. He saw only unhappiness waiting for him
there. Again, Steffens had created a hero in his self-image and
idealized the setting for greater effect. While he was not nearly as
big and athletic or as naive as Ditson, Steffens had a strikingly
similar experience at Berkeley. There he and his fictional character
part company. Instead of marrying his girl, Gussie Burgess, and
entering a business career after college, Steffens left for Europe and
eventually broke his engagement to Gussie. Steffens was not rejecting his past, but he was fearful of the consequences of returning
home. For Steffens, settling in New York was his opportunity to escape a predictable future.

These stories explained why Steffens was largely a failure as a fiction writer. His fiction usually fell into two categories. On the one
hand, he wrote often idyllic versions of his own childhood experiences. On the other hand, he composed thinly disguised accounts of his activities as a muckraker and journalist. His fiction
never developed any dramatic tension between the two. Personally,
he could not bring the innocent West of his childhood into contrast
with the vitality of industrial, polyglot, corrupt, urban America. His
contemporaries such as Frank Norris managed to do it; Steffens
could not. As a result, his fiction tended to be one dimensional. He
was more concerned with what was gained than with what was lost
in the process of experience.[5]

These characteristics of his fiction reflected his personal outlook.
In many respects, Steffens was a preeminently modern man. He
cared little for tradition or the past and its lessons. He believed in
the active life that meant total involvement in his environment. For
him, "New York was like a great swimming-hole into which every
day I dived . . . and swam around for something . . . worth getting." The trouble was that Steffens needed to tell everyone what
he had found immediately. This was fine for his newspaper stories
or journal articles, but it was a problem for his fiction. His short
stories were not usually the products of reflection, but were almost
visceral reactions to what he saw, heard, or felt. Although he tried
several times, he never successfully completed a novel. His impulse
to write came from his involvement in the world, and once he
removed himself from the action, he quickly lost his stimulus.[6]

At the same time, Steffens was the classic American innocent and would remain one his whole life. Steffens was always "unlearning" things—the central trait of American innocence. Throughout his career, he kept finding new worlds that promised a brighter future. The novelist takes his or her past experiences, ideas, and feelings and through the use of creative imagination forms a personal expression of his art. To begin anew continually would destroy the source of his or her creative impulse. The resultant work has currency and not complexity. This was true of Steffens. Everything he had to say was told in his articles or character sketches. There was little left for his fiction. Yet, these very same qualities made him a great journalist. This talent became immediately evident with his first job as a newspaper reporter with the venerable *New York Evening Post*.

This unexpected mixture of a Western young man by way of Europe, the most dynamic city in the nation, and a newspaper that represented nineteenth century liberal values proved to be a potent combination. With so many others of his time, Steffens found New York irresistible. Here was human drama from the grandest scale to the smallest detail. On Fifth Avenue, the barons of industry and finance were building mansions as monuments to themselves. Downtown, on the lower East Side, the new immigrants from southern and eastern Europe were scratching out an existence in the crowded, filthy tenements they were forced to call home. In between were the characters—the policeman, the politician, the crook—who gave the city its color. These were all subjects for the pen of the eager novice reporter.

Ironically, Steffens wrote for the most old-fashioned newspaper in the city. Under the guidance of Edward Lawrence Godkin, the *Post* was the bastion of mugwump politics. For Godkin, reform meant civil service, low tariff, Grover Cleveland, and opposition to Tammany Hall and its minions, the uneducated, unwashed masses. Conservative in layout as well as philosophy, the *Post* refused to make a spectacle of itself. Where the other papers had sensational headlines screaming across their front pages, the *Post* sedately presented facts and careful analyses of important events. For Godkin, who hated yellow journalism, the news did not include the reporting of crimes and the coverage of scandals. This was the perfect atmosphere for Steffens to begin his career. The *Post* was run by gentlemen, and Steffens was a gentleman and a rather conservative one at that. Under the direction of the city editor, Henry J. Wright, the young reporter learned how to write newspaper copy.

A healthy bargain was struck; the *Post* needed fresh blood and, in return, Steffens received an education.[7]

Beginning at space rates, Steffens soon graduated to a regular salary. He quickly demonstrated the two talents that made him a great reporter. He dug into the facts of a story and was never satisfied until he understood his subject or topic completely. And while investigating a story, he never lost sight of the human element. In truth, these were only different aspects of the single most important trait that dominated Steffens' career. Steffens needed to know fully and understand personally the world that was the subject for his pen. For other reporters, writing the news was simply a job; for Steffens it was an obsession. In this respect, Steffens was representative of a new type of journalism that was coming to the fore at the end of the last century.

Traditionally, powerful editors controlled the style and content of their newspapers. Reporters tended to be mechanics of the trade, more working class than middle class professionals. As Steffens observed them, they hurried to get their stories, wrote them, and then settled down to a leisurely game of cards. In the 1890s, this began to change rapidly as two new groups entered the scene. On the one hand, there were the reformers and political activists such as Jacob Riis and Abraham Cahan who were immigrants. They knew the ghetto and appreciated the often desperate conditions of life in urban, industrial America. At the other extreme were the young college graduates, mostly from Ivy League schools, who came to New York to find out something about life and write about it. These two diverse types had one important thing in common: Both had deep personal commitments to their subjects and their profession.[8]

By studying and reporting what he saw, Steffens was fulfilling several important goals. For one, he was making a success of himself. He was satisfying his ambitions for fame and fortune. Steffens very much enjoyed "this healthy American living, working and running." At the same time, his subject, New York, was an education in itself. He was learning the "complex, crude, significant but mixed facts of hard, practical life." The two things were inseparable from each other. Journalism offered Steffens the opportunity to observe and understand urban, industrial society as it replaced the America of his childhood. He was able to communicate his knowledge and to explain this often frightening new society to millions of Americans who were making the difficult adjustment to modern social realities. By performing this essential service, Steffens and many of his colleagues gained an almost indispensible place within the new culture. Steffens did not need to turn to his father's world, one that offered him no fresh opportunities. Instead, genteel America had to turn to its sons and daughters for advice and guidance. In the dawn of this new America, Steffens found a frontier of his own where he had identity, position, and, shortly, power.

At first, Steffens covered any minor story that needed a spare reporter. One of his early more or less regular assignments was to review the city's active German stage. Steffens was ideally suited for this work. He knew the language, was familiar with that culture's playwrights, and had some training within the German intellectual tradition. His reviews were urbane and facile, with a hint of snobbery. Criticizing one play, the young reporter commented that, "It is heavy where *it* ought to be light, and unnecessarily strained where it ought to run smoothly and naturally. . . . The stage-setting was uncommonly good, the play uncommonly poor." While his reviews were clear and concise, he could not resist showing off his knowledge of German philosophy and psychology. If Steffens had remained a critic, he certainly would have made an excellent one. Reviewing plays, however, never became more than a sidelight for him. His real work was in the streets.[9]

The first stop for Steffens was Wall Street, already the center of American corporate and financial power. Assigned to this "beat" at the beginning of the depression that would deeply scar the 1890s, Steffens little understood the whirlwind of events around him. He scarcely saw the misery that the panic of 1893 caused throughout the city and across the nation. His interest was in the bankers, brokers, and lawyers who were trying to control and take advantage of the situation. There was no hunger on Wall Street, only the excitement of fortunes being made and lost by the players of the game. With the excitement of the crash, Steffens forgot all about his plan to build a "scientific ethics" by objectively investigating the pattern of human behavior. Instead, he plunged into his new assignment with the verve and dedication that would mark all his journalism.

Always, his first step was to find out and meet the "inside" men who controlled Wall Street. Later, Steffens developed this pursuit into a fine art, but from the beginning he instinctively sought out the manipulators of power. Armed with a list of leading bankers and brokers, he began his financial education. Admitting his ignorance of Wall Street and banking, he asked each man to teach him the intricacies of stocks and corporate business. Somewhat to his surprise, with one exception, they willingly granted his request. After all, Steffens represented the *Post*, which certainly could be trusted with sensitive information. Steffens understood this special relationship and took great care not to damage it. When his sources tested him with information not for publication, Steffens made sure that the item did not appear in print. Slowly, these cautious sources took the young reporter into their confidence, enabling his paper to scoop its opposition.

Steffens had a simple method for exploiting his sources without betraying their trust. Warned in advance that a certain corporation was in serious difficulty, Steffens would research and write several columns about the company and then file them away. When the business finally did collapse, the *Post*, which often had the basic story already set in type, would have the news on the presses in a matter of moments. Consequently, Steffens gained a reputation as a financial reporter. In return for its favors, Wall Street reaped considerable benefits. For one thing, the *Post*'s objective and dull style of reporting such news, which Steffens had mastered, removed the sharp edge from even the most serious business reversal. The *Post* could make even a financial catastrophe sound like a matter of fact occurrence. Also, this guardian of fiscal restraint was an evening newspaper. Since bad news was inevitably released at the end of the trading day, the financial community had almost an entire day to digest and stabilize the situation. Without fully being aware of it, Steffens was successfully manipulated by his contacts for their own ends.[10]

Steffens did not care. He was caught up in the "joy of panic," and he had little interest in the consequences. More importantly, he was intrigued by the men who ran the American financial empire. He had escaped reading "what thinkers thought" and was seeing "what practical men did and why." He met J. Pierpont Morgan and even had the nerve to demand an explanation from the great banker about a news release that made no sense. While covering the financial district, the young reporter met the infamous James B. Dill, the corporate lawyer who made New Jersey a safe haven for big business and trusts. Laughing at Steffens' innocence, Dill explained the real "inside" story of corporate evasion of the law. The two men became fast friends and the rapidly maturing journalist never forgot what he learned from Dill.[11]

What Dill taught Steffens essentially had more to do with men and society than business and laws. Under the canny lawyer's guidance, Steffens learned the difference between an honest man and an intelligent one. It is impossible to understand much of what Steffens wrote without appreciating this distinction. For Steffens, the self-proclaimed honest man was little more than a righteous fool at best and a hypocrite at worst. Most men, especially businessmen, were in some ways corrupt, but they simply refused to recognize it. Too often, Steffens observed how good citizens justified their own immoral acts, but readily condemned others for lesser offenses. This was true of most of the men that Steffens met on Wall Street, but not of James B. Dill. His friend knew exactly what he was doing and the nature of the evil involved in his activities. With a hearty laugh and a twinkle in his eye, Dill admitted his own corruption and agreed that it should be stopped. This old lawyer was the "rightest" man Steffens had ever met, but not righteous. His honesty lay in his understanding of himself and the world around him and not in the spouting of superficial moral platitudes. At this early stage in his career, Steffens was unable to grasp the full implications of his discovery. He still had much to learn about the city and its people. [12]

If Wall Street exposed Steffens to the rich and powerful, the lower East Side showed him the teeming masses, the poor, and the immigrants. In part, the ghetto horrified him. The number and kinds of crimes were shocking testimonial to the chaos of the crowded streets. Soon, Steffens began to see crime as a part of the pattern of urban, immigrant life. He wrote of a particularly brutal murder as an illustration of both the desperation and the vitality of ethnic life. He described the music and play of a busy street in an Italian neighborhood being interrupted by the killing of a young woman. This bloody act threw the crowd into a rage that only subsided following the quick arrest of the murderer. In a matter of minutes, the street returned to normal. The children were again playing, the music resumed, and the "smiling" crowd was back to the business of the streets. The grotesque had become almost picturesque. [13]

Here Steffens nearly fell into the trap that caught so many students of ethnic life. As intellectuals, writers often felt themselves looking in on life and not living it. Even before their discovery of Freud's theories, many intellectuals saw themselves as overly moralized victims of a Puritan civilization. While they were chained to reflection, the immigrants, they thought, were instinctively reacting to the basic drives of life. Ironically, the envy of the intellectuals was based on their race and class consciousness. The immigrants enjoyed life because they were more primitive than the American middle class. Once civilized, the ethnics would curb their instincts. By romanticizing the immigrants, the writer-intellectual stereotyped them. In such literary portraits, the ghetto dwellers were not mature men and women struggling for existence and opportunity in a harsh world, but exotic children playing in a wonderfully strange environment. Although Steffens was, at times, guilty of these misconceptions, his writing usually demonstrated a deep understanding and appreciation of immigrant life in New York. [14]

Steffens fully recognized the dark side of life on the lower East Side. The housing of the poor was the greatest disgrace of the ghetto. Crowded together in slum tenements and once fashionable private homes, the immigrants lived with much filth and little privacy. To the horror of their mothers, small children watched the young prostitutes ply their trade. Describing the notorious tenement "the ship," which was finally being torn down, Steffens wrote, "It smells like the hold of an ancient slave ship, is leaky, dark, dismal, and ill ventilated." The saving virtue of the ghetto was obviously not in its houses but in the vitality of its varied people. [15]

In fact and thinly disguised fiction, Steffens described the characters and types of the ethnic neighborhoods. His articles told of the "thousands" of "drab, pale" young Jewish girls hurrying home in the gathering darkness from their jobs in the factory lofts and sweat shops. In the shadows, hiding their faces from passers-by, stood those who were broken by the hard life in the ghetto and spurned by their families and friends. In vignettes, the young journalist wrote of the tragedy of these failures, who became the human wreckage of the slums. Yet, Steffens was most impressed with the indomitable spirit of these people. He knew the "dark, handsome" young Italian, "big, strong, and bad," tamed and made a family man by a veritable "madonna" from Mulberry Bend. More often than not, Steffens' attempts at characterization were superficial and sentimental, and his ethnic short stories, after some success, failed to find a market. [16]

More substantial were Steffens' articles about the culture and ritual of various ethnic groups. In his "Leisure of the Poor," he argued that, "working people sometimes know best the pleasures of idleness." Perhaps because of his European experience, he understood the rich cafe society of the Germans, Austrians, and

Bohemians. He appreciated the "great stalwart laborers of Italy" who "when they have nothing to do they do nothing calmly and pleasantly." Seeing them "half awake, bathing in the sunlight on benches, stoops and on the sidewalks" did not mean that they were "mere loafers" but seasonal workers who enjoyed their free time. Nearby, their wives would "gossip on their haunches," watching their children as they played in the street. Steffens warned his readers not to judge these activities according to "your idea of living." Instead, they should recognize that these people "live out their lives in the indolent indulgence of a large capacity for enjoyment." Steffens sought to capture the full panorama of life in these hectic streets. From his pen came accounts of everything from small personal tragedies to grand neighborhood festivals.[17]

Despite their poverty, the immigrants continued to celebrate the holidays of their native lands. Steffens found the Italians especially adept at making their ramshackled streets into colorful settings for their festivals. In the *Post*, Steffens described the feast of St. Donato.

A rear tenement was draped to concealment with the sheets and bedspreads, quilts and banners, white, pink, blue, yellow, and green, plain or with embroidered flowers, figures, and diagrams, some with gold pasteboard decorations. The steps of the tenement and the porch were the foundation of the altar which rose to the top of the second-story window, where, calm and small, perched the figure of Saint Donato in white robes with spangles and plenty of jewelry.

Steffens was a keen enough observer not to confuse the occasion with any special religiosity. He reported in the same story that the sponsors of the festival kept the saint's statue in a saloon to prevent the parish priest from charging for its use every year.[18]

Steffens saved some of his best writing and greatest affection for the immigrant Jews of the lower East Side. He became so fascinated with the Hebrew religion that he practiced many of its rites and customs. In "Yom Kipper on the East Side," Steffens described that most important of high holy days in loving detail. Before sunset, there was a flurry of activity as shopkeepers closed their shops and "girls and young clerks darted out and hurried away down the streets." Hester Street was deserted except for a "few fruit-peddlers" who sold the last of their apples "with one hand on the handle, in the nervous attitude of going." In the synagogue, some men were already "swaying gently, earnestly, back and forward as

they mumble, reading the book of prayer, and tapped their chest."
With the beggars grouped at the door, the services began with "the
ancient and beautiful" chants of this most persecuted of all
peoples.[19]

As touching and memorable as Steffens found all this, he
recognized that the old culture and practices were giving way in the
new world of New York. Not far from the synagogue were "a lot of
unclean, sullen, dark visage Jews in wretched clothes," who had
gathered "to mock their race and religion." These young men and
women "slunk" into a rented hall where "to break the law of
Moses, [they] smoked cigarettes, drank beer and feasted on apples."
Their elders could do little to save their children. They could only
tear at their hair, rip their garments, and cry out in total despair.
Some found such scenes comical, but Steffens understood this
"tragic conflict." Long before Margaret Mead, Steffens recognized
the growing gap between the first and second generations of immigrants. The old clung to tradition; the young rejected their
parents' ways and accepted the values of this new land. This meant
the end of thousands of years of "continuous devotion, courage and
suffering for a cause." Throughtout his career, Steffens continued
to have a special understanding and sympathy for cultures that were
different from his own.[20]

For all its pain and suffering, the ghetto did not depress Steffens,
but elated him. The same could be said for Wall Street during the
panic of the 1890s. For Steffens, these situations and conditions
were far from tragedies, but exciting opportunities. Steffens was not
as insensitive to the plight of the urban poor as he was simply preoc-
cupied with the possibilities of life in the metropolis. The dynamic
city was the source of adventure and knowledge for this "nice,
original American boob" as Steffens called himself. His stories and
articles made his reputation as a journalist. Godkin even asked his
young star reporter to take the editorship of a small newspaper in
Connecticut. Steffens refused, hoping to become the city editor of
the *Post*. While he waited for the offer that would never come,
Steffens became a pivotal figure in one of the grand crusades to expose police and political corruption and reform New York.[21]

CHAPTER 2

Crooks, Cops, and the Commissioner

I N late 1893, Steffens accepted the new *Post* position at police headquarters on Mulberry Street in lower Manhattan. His
feelings about the assignment were ambiguous to say the least. "It
is beastly work," he told his father, "police, criminals and low-
browed 'heelers' in the vilest part of the horrible East side amid
poverty, sin and depravity." Steffens was concerned that such conditions might "degrade" him. At the same time, the young journalist believed that there was the equal chance that the work
"would make a man of me." But all these considerations were
secondary to the young newspaperman's ambitions. Ironically,
Steffens saw this terrible environment that was a crushing burden to
so many as his opportunity for success. To him, the *Post*'s police
bureau was "my field, my chance."[1]

Fortunately, his mentor in his new assignment was a man who
tempered Steffens' apparently callous ambition with understanding.
Jacob Riis, a Danish immigrant, was the veteran police reporter for
the *New York Evening Sun*. Author of *How The Other Half Lives*, a
brilliant description of conditions in the ghetto, Riis taught his willing student that "a suicide, a fire, a murder" was not only a crime
or a catastrophe but also a human interest story. Most of all, he
showed his protégé that a reporter was more than a passive observer
of events. The true journalist was an investigator who was never
satisfied until he found the causes of a disaster. What Riis saw on
the streets of New York turned him into a reformer who "worked
through despair to set the wrong right." When he discovered that
the city's water supply was polluted, he demanded and got a
cleaner system. He cried out against the slum tenements and saw
dozens of those wretched, dangerous buildings torn down. Already
inclined in this direction, Steffens would emulate his teacher and
eventually surpass him.[2]

Steffens quickly learned to look behind the crime for the story.

27

He wrote with poignancy and humor about both crimes and the criminals. The terrible knife murder of a young woman became a sympathetic description of Italian character and life in the ghetto. The clumsy clubbing of strikers by inexperienced policemen became a dissertation by an older patrolman on the proper method of using the night stick. A murder investigation became a portrait of a typical day at a neighborhood police station. The confession of a young black man to murder interrupts the sleepy quiet of a hot afternoon. The excitement draws a crowd, and the police entertain their audience by cruelly ridiculing their suspect. Investigating the crime, they find that the confessed killer had missed his intended victim and they release him. The station and the streets return to business as usual.[3]

At the same time, Steffens recognized that there was more to his beat than human interest and mood pieces. The ghetto produced something besides picturesque Italians and delightful street scenes. It was also the breeding ground for the criminal. He found it almost impossible to accurately describe the "vileness of the physical conditions of tenement life." There, a boy grew up "with the ambition to become a notorious burglar." Young girls dreamed of careers as "dancers and concert-hall singers." The middle class reader knew well that these were code words for prostitute. Steffens, belaboring the point, assured his readers that there would be no "domestic life" for these girls but only "money for pretty clothes." Despite their Victorian tone, such articles saw social conditions rather than race or depravity as the causes of crime.[4]

As he came to know the thief and the pickpocket, Steffens wrote of them with sympathy, wit, and irony. He recognized that many criminals were artists, professional men with an enormous pride in their craft. He took glee in telling the tale of how a patrolman unwittingly helped two clever burglars load stolen merchandise on their truck. Most importantly, Steffens discovered that these men, condemned by society, often exhibited praiseworthy traits. They were, more often than not, honorable men with strong characters. This was to be a significant theme in Steffens' writing for the remainder of his career.[5]

In fiction as well as fact, Steffens insisted that society confused social standing with virtue and integrity. In his short story, " 'Ashes?' A Dock Rat," a boat thief meets a stockbroker in a highly contrived situation. While sneaking aboard a yacht, Ashes, the thief, is surprised by its owner. The two men begin to talk, and Ashes is fascinated by the stockbroker. When a waterfront gang attacks the vessel during their conversation, the cunning Ashes helps the wealthy man repulse the assault. Given the opportunity to reciprocate, the stockbroker turns his back on his benefactor. In this obvious way, the whole point of the story is to show how appearances can be deceiving. The supposed scoundrel proves to be courageous and a man of his word. The bastion of society has no scruples and acts only according to his own self-interest. Steffens believed that this kind of contradiction permeated American society. Too often, the good men were really the bad men and vice versa. Steffens found this to be especially true of the police.[6]

If the "low life" interested Steffens, the police enthralled him. Assigned to cover the Reverend Charles H. Parkhurst and his Society for the Prevention of Crime, Steffens was introduced to the criminality of those who were supposedly the guardians of the law. The good minister's crusade was directed against vice and its protection for a price by the police. His wrath focused on the saloon, the prostitute, and the gambling house. Steffens, who was very much a genteel reformer, immediately joined the cause. He was soon reporting to the public how the police were the center of a system of corruption that extended into every dark corner of New York. Arriving at police headquarters for the first time, Steffens promised to remain a police reporter until "Clubber" Williams, an infamously corrupt police captain, was removed from the force.[7]

Despite his ardor for reform, Steffens simply could not hide his pleasure and excitement with his job. In his *Autobiography*, Steffens recounted how "reporting at police headquarters was like a college education in this, that one had to take several courses all together." The only difference was that, unlike his formal education, he was "interested in each of these courses." His assignment taught him "life as it is lived." For all his indignation over corruption and crime, he was obviously intrigued with the "complex, crude, significant but mixed facts of hard practical life." The dark side of society was a shining light to the young newspaperman. This was reflected in his stories and articles and saved him from the overbearing self-righteousness that he so detested in others.[8]

Steffens never vilified or condemned the average policeman, whom he saw as a victim of the system. He characterized the rank and file police officer as a bluff, sometimes cruel, but basically good-natured Irishman or German. When Steffens described his failings, he did it in sympathetic and often humorous terms. In

"Betrayed by His Horse," he told how the "shrewd" mounted policemen assigned to a semirural precinct in the Bronx escaped their duty. Riding out on patrol, they would rendezvous deep in the woods at a barn well-stocked with drink, food, and women. Suspicious of his men, the precinct captain borrowed the horse of a "keen old" patrolman and let the animal have its head. Without missing a step, the horse took its rider to the barn, exposing the offenders. The guilty men were not dismissed from the force but disciplined and returned to patrol.[9]

Such a story was indicative of Steffens' deep middle class bias at this point in his life. Steffens saw both crooks and cops as essentially working class types. They were shrewd and street-wise but not particularly bright. As men who routinely followed orders, they participated in the corruption of the city, but were not responsible for it. Like the immigrants, the police were children who knew no better and therefore should not be punished severely for their indiscretions. The mounted patrolmen were similar to boys playing hooky from school. When caught by responsible authorities, they should be scolded for their prank—a fitting punishment for an adolescent crime. There was more than a hint of condescension in Steffens' affection and amusement. In many respects, he did not take these men seriously. Without strong guidance and leadership, he did not expect the working class policeman to adhere to the same ethical standards of conduct that were obligatory for his class.

For Steffens, the real evil lay in the "system" and those men who controlled it. He was one of the first journalists or social critics of any kind, for that matter, to realize the profound truth that crime was "a part of the police system." Steffens meant this in two different and distinct ways. As professionals, the police and the criminals recognized each others' skills. After all, they were both part of the same business. Between the law and the law breaker there was an agreed upon code of acceptable behavior, and each side abided by the rules of the game. Steffens had little quarrel with this aspect of the system and even saw some social benefits in this arrangement. Yet, this "demiworld" also operated on a much more pernicious level. Here the police actively "protected" and often encouraged the illegal activities of the underworld. In return, the police received a percentage of the illicit profit on vice, gambling, and prostitution. This was the "price" that criminals paid for their cooperation. This "system" was the "business" of "perverts," politicians, and police captains.[10]

At the center of corruption in New York was Tammany Hall and its political allies within both the Republican and Democratic parties. These leaders and their followers trafficked in the spoils of office and the profits of vice. Steffens was more concerned with exposing the "sachems" than the Indians of the Democratic machine. The "bosses" were the ones responsible for the corruption of the city, its politics, and the police force. Steffens was sure that the system was completely dependent on its leaders for its prosperity. Rid New York of these men and the city would have lean, efficient government. The sophistication of Steffens' analysis ended when he arrived at solutions.

Again, Steffens looked to his middle class heritage for answers. Before the municipal elections of 1894, which would sweep the Republican reform ticket into office, Steffens declared himself a "mugwump independent." Partisanship, he felt, was the greatest evil in American politics. In New York, it enabled the bosses of the two parties, but especially the Democrats, to control the political process and corrupt the management of government. Analyzing the successful election of the reform ticket, Steffens saw "a steady growth here among intelligent men of a belief in the righteousness of non-partisan political action." If this "independent vote" continued to grow as Steffens hoped, he was confident that corrupt party politics would eventually go down to final defeat.[11]

Within this genteel, mostly Republican tradition, Steffens, with Godkin's blessing, hammered away at Tammany in his articles. In alliance with the Reverend Parkhurst, he sought to expel the "proven corruption" of the Democratic machine from municipal office. In its place, the Republican party selected the best citizens to reform the government. The task, as Steffens later recalled it, was simply "to discharge the bad men and elect good men." William L. Strong, a prominent businessman and neophyte politician, was easily elected mayor, and the "good men" had their opportunity to put their theories into action.[12]

For Steffens, the new administration's true test would be to clean up the police department. Even before the victory at the polls, Steffens gloated over the growing discomfort of the Tammany "gang" that directed and profited from police corruption. As the results of the election became apparent, Steffens gleefully reported the "irritability" of such men as James J. Martin, president of the Board of Police and notorious Democratic boss. Martin and his cohorts were being forced out "to make way for decent public officials." This was accomplished in the police department by the appointment of a bipartisan Board of Police Commissioners. Steffens got even more than he bargained for: Theodore Roosevelt became the head of the four man board.[13]

For the next twenty years, the lives and careers of Steffens and Roosevelt were constantly intertwined. When they met, there were already several striking similarities between them. Both were highly successful young men with bright futures. Each had chosen to make his mark on the world in rather unorthodox ways. This, of course, was especially true of the older Roosevelt. Born into the American aristocracy, Roosevelt had selected an unlikely career in politics. Yet he was much more than a patrician politician. A rancher, reformer, and naturalist, he was also a respected writer and historian. Like so many others, Steffens was captivated by the dynamic personality and often gargantuan excesses of the future Rough Rider and president.

Roosevelt was more than a friend to Steffens; he also became the focus and catalyst for one of the most important themes in Steffens' writing. Throughout his career, Steffens was fascinated by the strong man in public life. Roosevelt was the first and a preeminent example of this type. Here was a man who left others literally gasping for breath as he took on the challenge of reforming the police department. Because of his background and his own personality, Roosevelt could have been a "brilliant social success" or made a "large fortune." Instead, unlike so many men of wealth and talent, Roosevelt chose the active life and a "career of public service."[14]

In the early stages of their relationship, Roosevelt filled two needs for the young reporter. For one, the new police commissioner took command of the situation. To this point, the only men that Steffens knew who controlled their destinies and surroundings were leaders such as James Dill. As much as he admired them, Steffens knew that they were working against the public good. Roosevelt was not only "independent" and "fearless," he was devoted to the "struggle for principle." At last, Steffens had his example of what good men could be. He recognized that Roosevelt, for all his enormous energy and activity, was calculating and thoughtful. He lived in the real world, but remained committed to its improvement and not simply to his own aggrandizement. Eventually, Steffens' faith in the morality of good men would disappear, but he would always retain his admiration for strong ones.[15]

At the same time, Roosevelt's friendship gave Steffens a position near the center of growing power. Steffens, with so many of his intellectual and literary contemporaries, was horrified at the prospect of becoming a passive observer of events. As Roosevelt's informal adviser and his confidant as governor of New York and then president of the United States, Steffens was "inside" the corridors of power. He felt none of the impotence of intellectuals who had no hand in the shaping of public policy. Because of this relationship, Steffens' articles about Roosevelt and his programs took on a public importance. In fact, however, these stories revealed little new about Roosevelt, his ideas, or his proposals. In many respects, Steffens' columns, especially those written during Roosevelt's successful quest for the governorship, were little more than campaign literature for his friend. Nevertheless, Steffens' articles could not be ignored because there was always the possibility that he might disclose something new and important about Roosevelt. Steffens was aware of this, and he carefully dangled this possibility before his readers.

In his *Autobiography*, Steffens recalled, probably with some exaggeration, just how pivotal a role he played in Roosevelt's efforts to clean up the police department. He and Riis taught the ignorant new commissioner all about crime, cops, and corruption. Once they managed to get the recently appointed, eager Roosevelt calmed down, the two reporters described "the situation to him, telling him which higher officers to consult, which to ignore and punish; what the forms were, the customs, the rules, methods." By educating Roosevelt, they turned his vast energy loose on the corrupt department. Roosevelt went swiftly to work. As the highly satisfied Steffens looked on, the new commissioner fired "Clubber" Williams. He disciplined and dismissed crooked officers and rewarded the honest ones. Patroling the streets in a disguise that could not hide his prominent features and therefore fooled no one, Roosevelt made sure that the law was being enforced by the cops on the beat. Eventually, he convinced the skeptical police that he was an "honest man, an honest police commissioner." For Steffens, this was Roosevelt's most important contribution to reform. He was fair and straight with the police and proved that the system could operate honestly and without illegitimate "pull." [16]

Despite such accomplishments, Mayor Strong and the reform ticket were soundly defeated by Tammany's slate in the next election, and Steffens searched for the reasons. His explanation marked the first glimpse of the mature social critic who would write *The

Shame of the Cities. From the beginning, Steffens wondered if the reformers had the "intellect and energy" to maintain control of the government. He quickly recognized that Mayor Strong would be incapable of running a nonpartisan and effective administration. He had no "strong trait" and was too weak to put principle above himself and his party. Instead, he distributed the patronage and spoils of office "in a more or less equitable division . . . modified by resentments and prejudices, with just a sly touch of ambition to be the next Governor of the State." The rest of the reformers were "not accustomed to the details of party management" and failed to know "when to touch the crowds." In short, they were amateurs, and it was only a matter of time before the professionals would regain office. Tammany's victory proved Steffens' analysis to be all too accurate, and never again would Steffen consider joining any reform movement that lacked strong, knowledgeable leaders. [17]

Steffens shared the lessons that he learned from this experience with his readers. In his "As to Police Reform," written in 1902, he analyzed the mistakes that he and others had made in New York. Although some might "laugh" at him, Steffens still believed that "a corrupt police force can be reformed." In other words, many of his ideas were not changed by the defeat of the reformers. While he would have denied it, much of his argument was only a sophisticated rehashing of the traditional methods of reform; men of character must throw out the rascals. Leadership by "an honest man who knows the police" was the "one requisite" for effective reform. Policemen "must be compelled" to do their duty by this willful hand. At the same time, "the higher officers who have become habitual criminals" must be removed from their posts. The Reverend Parkhurst would have agreed wholeheartedly with all this. [18]

On the other hand, Steffens did offer some original observations and suggestions that would shock the sensibilities of his audience. He was sure that the police should not be made to crack down on all vice. The effort to do just that in New York had "failed ignominiously." According to Steffens, the reason was obvious. The salaries of policemen, especially the cops on the beat, were too small. The criminals paid the police more not to enforce the law than the cities did to arrest them. At the same time, the people who demanded these statutes were the very ones who cried out against their enforcement. It was the "business men of New York" who most opposed the closing of saloons and the end of gambling and prostitution. It would, they claimed, be bad for business. [19]

Consequently, Steffens placed much of the blame for the failure of reform, not on the criminals and the police, but on the good, law-abiding citizens of the city. In their "Anglo-Saxon hypocrisy," they demanded enforcement of the laws and, yet, screamed when they received it. End police corruption, he warned, and "you will have clergymen . . . bankers and lawyers, doctors and, of course, politicians, in your office, defending and protecting the crooked cops." Steffens realized that "crime was a business" and as such was an integral part of American life. There was profit in vice, and any disturbance threatened the whole of the business system. As the young reporter saw it, only when society stopped encouraging selfish behavior for profit could it expect the police to be cleansed of corruption.[20]

The belief that good men were responsible for evil was typical of Steffens' use of irony in both his journalism and fiction. He was fascinated with personal and social paradoxes. Even his own dress and demeanor suggested this. Steffens, the reformer, the radical, the bohemian, usually wore rather formal, old-fashioned garb, typical of his father's genteel America. He had a neatly groomed goatee that contrasted with his unorthodox Roman emperor hair style. Certainly, the paradoxes went deeper. He professed a distaste for business, but did very well in the stock market and speculated successfully in real estate. He recognized that titular heads of corporations were just that, figureheads for powerful bosses who operated behind the scenes. Still, at one point, Steffens was tempted to take such a position himself. Perhaps the greatest irony of these years was his career as a journalist. He became a success by describing the misfortunes and exposing the corruption of society. Later in his life, Steffens would recognize these contradictions, and this would contribute mightily to his *Autobiography*. Already at the turn of the century, a sense of irony was an integral part of his style.

Steffens used, often overused, the ironic twist in his short stories. In "The Man That Knows," the Honorable Wortley Bordon becomes a powerful figure in a political machine because of his vast knowledge of the organization's misdeeds. He is made police chief and uses his post to gather further damning information about everyone, including the reformer who is working to throw Bordon and his gang out of office. Threatened with defeat, the police chief only has to release the facts to cause a scandal that will turn the tide. He cannot do it. Bordon has guarded his secrets so closely that he has become a "miser," willing to lose power for the sake of his precious information. The use of irony is so heavy that all else in the story is sacrificed to it. Instead of using this literary device to illuminate his characters, Steffens made them its pawns. As a result, Steffens' characters seldom developed into interesting, lively people dealing with believable situations.[21]

In "The Banker's Love Story," published by *Ainslee's* in 1902, the chief character, Francis P. Jewett, is an apparently powerful banker. In reality, he is only a front for the aristocratic Wall Street financier, Chester Frewan. The banker, "a querulous, fretful little man," burns with jealousy and hatred for his boss. From this point, the story quickly degenerates into an imitation of O. Henry without that author's sentimentality. Seeking revenge for constant slights and humiliations, Jewett arranges for the unsuspecting and lonely Frewan to meet and fall in love with a governess. Everything goes as planned but, predictably, the tale ends with an ironic twist. The governess turns out to be beautiful and sophisticated and for a wedding present her employers, who treat her as a daughter, give the newlyweds a castle. Again the lackey, the banker is forced to make the arrangements for the purchase of the gift. It is a cute tale with a surprise ending and that is all that can be said about it. The same cannot be said of Steffens' newspaper articles.[22]

When dealing with social reality, Steffens' use of irony had a different effect. With its humor in sharply drawn vignettes, he told poignant truths about municipal politics. The "novel candidate" who took the civil service exam and actually "showed a definite knowledge of his prospective duties" said more about patronage under Tammany than could any long, scholarly article. On a more profound level, Steffens outlined a whole series of social-political paradoxes in the years before he went to *McClure's*. Good men are the source of evil. Dishonest men tell the truth. Good citizens want bad government; or bad men make good leaders. These apparent contradictions were powerful perceptions of social reality and not products of Steffens' imagination. They were shockingly real, and they exploded many of the myths that Americans held about themselves and about their governments and politics.[23]

CHAPTER 3

Shameful Facts

THE ambitious Steffens, dissatisfied with what he considered his slow rate of advancement at the *Post*, became the city editor of the *Commercial Advertiser* in 1897. In four years he turned this "wretched, old street walker" of a newspaper into a lively young lady. Detesting the conventional style of journalism, Steffens fired his veteran reporters and replaced them with young writers who had little or no professional experience. To attract such fresh talent, Steffens turned the *Advertiser* into an unorthodox school of journalism with himself as headmaster. From Harvard, Yale, and the other Ivy League schools came the likes of Finley Peter Dunn and Hutchin Hapgood, eager to write and ready to take part in Steffens' experiment. To add balance and wisdom to the proceedings, Steffens hired Abraham Cahan, novelist, social realist, and radical socialist. Late into the night Steffens, Cahan, and the young staff would discuss art, theatre, politics, and the ghetto. Steffens wanted them to write as they talked and lived, with the verve and excitement of discovery. Their subject was New York: "rich and poor, wicked and good, ugly but beautiful, growing great." He demanded no particular style, and the only literary sin was dullness. With these standards, Steffens and his colleagues made the *Commercial Advertiser* into an interesting, successful newspaper. But, with profits came conservatism, and by 1901, the owners had changed the *Advertiser* into a safe, conventional journal.[1]

Too tired to resist and with the challenge gone, Steffens heeded the call of Samuel S. McClure. The eccentric, dynamic McClure was gathering a brilliant staff of journalists at his magazine and he wanted Steffens for his managing editor. The idea was good, but the results were bad. It soon became clear to both men that Steffens was more an inspiration than an editor. In one of his flashing moments of genius, McClure ordered Steffens out of the office and into the world. Freed from the drudgery of management, Steffens traveled from city to city looking for fresh stories and new talent. He quickly found what he wanted in the politics and corruption of municipal government. Having assigned a local journalist to write an article on St. Louis, Steffens was dissatisfied with the results and redid the piece to give it more bite. From the start, Steffens recognized the potential of the topic. He excitedly announced to Ida Tarbell that a series about urban corruption and reform "would make my name." Consequently, Steffens decided to write all the articles himself.[2]

As Steffens expected, the series caused a national sensation. He had gone to the Middle West searching for material that would sell magazines. This was his job, and he had no qualms about it. As early as 1897, he recognized that his field was dominated by the "commercial spirit." Therefore, journalists must have a "distinct appreciation for the power of opinion." This approach now paid off for Steffens. Feeling the public pulse, he had discovered, not created, the interest in municipal graft and reform. His articles proved to be so popular that they were collected into a book, *The Shame of the Cities*. For this Steffens did little rewriting, correctly insisting that the articles were and should remain "journalism." With the series for *McClure's* and the subsequent book, Steffens made a name for himself by feeding the new and hearty American appetite for national news.[3]

This was a near revolutionary change in the nature of journalism and communications. Traditionally, the reading public received only local publications that carried the national news in the form of dry releases from the news services. There had always been a few national magazines, but they appealed to an essentially elite or scholarly clientele. Until the emergence of inexpensive, popular magazines such as *McClure's*, the only source of national opinion making had been the political parties. Their orators, editors, and organizations shaped and slanted the news to fit their party's political and ideological needs. Steffens and the other muckraking journalists changed all this. They offered an alternative to the nation. Steffens' exposé made local news national, and he gave it his own political perspective. This combination marked the beginning of political muckraking.

Yet, the form was as important as the focus in explaining the popularity of the series. Although he needed little advice, Steffens followed McClure's guidelines for good, effective journalism. Articles should be exciting—even shocking—readable, and realistic.

The Shame of the Cities was all these things and more. Each install-ment was a detective story, telling the secret and nefarious dealings of crooks, politicians, corporations, and supposedly upstanding citizens. In every city, the exposure of corruption was followed almost inevitably by a titanic battle between the "boodlers" and the reformers. There was the drama of heroic men confronting a power-ful, pertinacious enemy in the courts and at the polls. The articles were all the more exciting and important because they were real; Steffens had the facts.[4]

As a journalist, Steffens knew exactly what to do and what not to do with his information. For his articles, he did not "gather with in-difference all the facts and arrange them patiently for permanent preservation for laboratory analysis." He was neither a scientist nor a historian. The scholar was responsible for all the facts, only judg-ing them as to their importance in the overall scheme of his study. Steffens, the journalist, based his use of facts on quite different criteria. For one thing, he recognized that certain facts had an in-trinsic quality that made them naturally interesting to an audience. Such facts might be exciting, new, of current concern, or unex-pected. In this case, Steffens had found "shameful facts," and he shocked his audience with them. In and of themselves, the presence of these facts in his articles made them a popular item.[5]

Steffens was not satisfied with this. He readily manipulated his facts to intensify further their impact. Often discarding nine-tenths of his information, he marshaled the selected material into devastating portrayals of municipal corruption. He named names, dates, and amounts of bribes, bargains, and payoffs. Steffens appeared almost irresponsible with his allegations but there were the carefully chosen facts to support his charges. In "The Shame of Minneapolis," he described how the elected officials and police of that city supported, even encouraged, vice and crime for a fee. For proof, he offered the facsimile of a page from "the Big Mit Ledger," an account of regularly scheduled payoffs by crooked gamblers to the mayor, police chief, and detectives. Such revelations caused a sensation but, to Steffens, were not sensational. He did it all for the purpose of uncovering "the civic pride of an ap-parently shameless citizenship."[6]

For Steffens, the essence of investigative journalism was not in the discovery of new facts or even the exposure of wrongdoing. He did not want simply to provide information; he wanted to "move and convince" the public of the true character of the situation.

Steffens saw an acute difference between the two. The first only connoted knowledge, the second, action. This was the "journalism of it." His goal was "to see if the shameless facts, spread out in all their shame, would not burn through our civic shamelessness and set fire to American pride." Steffens' careful selection of his material was not the act of the disinterested observer but that of the passionate advocate of reform. In each of the articles, his moral indignation at the facts of corruption was obvious. He scolded and dared the American people to answer his facts and end the corruption of their cities. As he admitted to his audience, "I did not want to preserve, I wanted to destroy the facts."[7]

Steffens' method of inducing reform appeared to be startlingly unorthodox. He placed the blame for the failure of local government squarely on the shoulders of the citizenry. Steffens boldly pronounced that "The misgovernment of the American people is misgovernment by the American people." Americans were not "innocent" but "corruptible." The decline of municipal government could be traced directly to the "moral weakness" of the average citizen. Misdeeds in "public affairs" were only extensions of what Americans practiced in their "private concerns." Steffens detected "no essential difference between the pull that gets your wife into society or for your book a favorable review, and that which gets a heeler into office, a thief out of jail. . . ." He had no patience with the usual excuses given for the corruption of local government. They were only "hypocritical lies that save us from clear sight of ourselves." Here is the key to understanding exactly how Steffens expected reform to come about.[8]

If the journalistic means were new, the formula was as old as America itself. His articles were the first step in a moral dialectic that Steffens surely believed would inevitably lead to the desired result. The initial step was to "shame" the American people into admitting their guilt. By the very act of recognizing their sinfulness, the people were being forced to "save" themselves. This was the heart of the process. The "disgraceful confession" led to moral indignation that became a "declaration of honor." The conclusion followed automatically from the dialectic. Once "aroused," the people "ceased to be spectators" of their own immorality. The now "determined and active" citizenry had no choice but to cleanse themselves of their corruption.[9]

In part, Steffens' articles were so well received because he spoke the language of Christian politics. Like his audience, he was a nineteenth century moral-political man, confronted with a mysterious new age. In his analysis, Steffens was modern enough to do away with the overt theology of evangelical politics, substituting shame for sin and pride for salvation. Still, his moral meaning was clear to his audience. With him, they agreed that there was an integral connection between individual redemption and social reform. The good man was the concerned citizen, responsible for both his own moral character and that of his community. As Steffens proudly noted in the "Introduction" to *The Shame of the Cities*, the favorable reaction of the people to his series was proof that they could "stand the truth" of his accusations. In fact, it is more evidence of Steffens' creative genius as a social observer and journalist.

Steffens explained emerging twentieth century realities with nineteenth century rhetoric and concepts. There were deep tensions as a result. Many of the new conditions did not easily fit into traditional perspectives. Because of this, Steffens often distorted his subject and passed the misconceptions on to his audience. At least partially adhering to the genteel reform tradition, his solutions tended to be simplistic. Nevertheless, Steffens did provide a means for his readers to understand much about urban, industrial America. He recognized that the corporation was replacing the entrepreneur as the symbol of American business. He glimpsed the truth that cities were more than small towns grown large. He developed symbols, signs, and systems that made this rapidly changing society intelligible to those who lived within it. He helped replace confusion with understanding, chaos with complexity.

First, Steffens sought to dispel the myths Americans held about the nature of corruption in their cities. Many blamed the immigrants for the immorality of municipal government. Untutored in the ways of democracy, they were the ignorant tools of the big city machines. Steffens quickly discounted this argument. True, St. Louis was German, and Minneapolis, Scandinavian, and both had corrupt governments. Yet, the latter city was ruled by New Englanders, not the immigrants. Philadelphia, "the purest American community of all," was the worst governed as well. On the other hand, the two most successful reform movements were in the "mongrel bred" cities of New York and Chicago. Other critics found the cause of corruption in the young age of American urban centers. With maturity, they thought, American cities would follow the example of their better managed counterparts in Europe, es-

pecially in Germany. If this was so, Steffens asked, why did
Philadelphia boodlers divide "their graft in unison with the ancient
chime of Independence Hall [?]" None of these reasons would do,
and Steffens readily pointed his accusing finger at the real
culprits.[10]

With harsh bluntness, Steffens announced that "in all cities, the
better class—the business men—are the sources of corruption." The
blanket condemnation was not nearly as terrible as it first appeared
to be. Like so many of his fellow reformers and muckrakers,
Steffens made an important distinction between the average
businessman, the entrepreneur, and the big businessman. The
"typical business man" was a "bad citizen" because he was too
"busy" to involve himself in the "unwelcome duties of citizenship."
This was the crime of "neglect," not active, personal corruption.
Such a man was only guilty of permitting the creation and growth
of bad government. In the end, he was as much a victim of corrupt
government as any other citizen. Steffens directed his scorn at the
big businessman, who was a "self-righteous fraud," directly responsible for the sad state of his own cities.[11]

As the articles appeared in *McClure's Magazine*, the story was
always the same. In St. Louis, the corruption went deep, but it
began at the "top." Enticed by public franchises, "influential
citizens, capitalists and great corporations" sought to loot their city.
With their special privileges granted by bribery and graft, these
"big men" stood behind the "boodlers" and supported the
"looters." Pittsburgh was much like St. Louis. Corruption began
"above," with the railroads bribing public officials to gain access to
the terminals of that city. Quickly, the political machine found out
just how "cheap" it was to buy the businessman. Public fund
deposits were "enough for the average banker." Merchants and
manufacturers "were kept well in hand by many little municipal
grants and privileges." Confronted with reform, these corporation
presidents, bankers, and financiers could not stand the idea. When
it came to Chicago, "they rose up, purple in the face, and cursed
reform." While the return of clean, efficient government would
benefit the community, it would "hurt their business." Consequently, they fought the reformers with threats, bribes, and intimidation. Again and again, Steffens emphasized that his litany
was the song of most cities. Municipal corruption was an American
way of life and Steffens knew exactly why.[12]

Politics was business, and business was the pursuit of self-interest.

For Steffens, "The commercial spirit is the spirit of profit, not patriotism . . . of individual gain, not national prosperity; of trade and dickering, not principle." This idea did not originate with Steffens. It was as old as the Puritans and as young as the progressives. Democratic government was representative government where elected officials served the desires and needs of the whole community. When manufacturers and bankers made government into a business, "public spirit became private spirit, public enterprise became private greed." Gone was the politics of civic virtue and, in its place, was the politics of selfish gain. The politician was no more than "a business man with a speciality." Through bribery, he sold his services to the highest bidder. This was government "by the rascals, for the rich." Echoing the words of District Attorney Joseph Folk of St. Louis, Steffens argued that this was "no ordinary felony, but treason." Government by oligarchy, representing the special interests, was overthrowing American democracy.[13]

What is missing from Steffens' analysis of this phenomenon of business corruption of government is the reason for its appearance at the end of the nineteenth century. He recognized that it was "new," but he did not know why. If he had examined his own articles a little more carefully, he would have discovered the cause. In each case, the cities he investigated had become corrupted by business as these once small towns became urban industrial centers. Steffens admitted that St. Louis businessmen had once ruled their community well. With "pluck, intelligence, and tremendous energy," they had built a large, powerful city. This demanded new streets, water systems, lighting, and transit networks. The previously unheard of profits in these public services created "greedy business men and bribers." In Pittsburgh, railroads and local transit began the process. Corruption had been "occasional and criminal till the first great corporations made it businesslike and respectable." With the growth of capital and industry, municipal corruption had increased "naturally." With all this evidence, Steffens could only vividly describe what he did not yet quite understand.[14]

Steffens did know that there was a "system" to the corruption of local government. Everywhere, graft, bribery and looting took the same form. This pattern was not "accidental," but "the impersonal effect of natural causes." In his series, Steffens made each city represent some phase of this organized corruption. St. Louis was the best example of boodle. Minneapolis had made police graft a lucrative enterprise. Pittsburgh had a political and industrial machine that controlled every aspect of community life. Philadelphia was so contented with general civic corruption that its citizens had given away their right to vote. They all had one thing in common. In every city, there was a single man, the boss, who controlled the system. As Steffens put it, "when anything extraordinary is done in American municipal politics, whether for good or evil, you can trace it inevitably to one man. The people do not do it. Neither do the 'gangs,' 'combines,' or political parties. They are but instruments by which bosses . . . rule the people."[15]

Although he was one of their bitterest foes, Steffens rather liked the bosses as men. They were intelligent, often generous, and usually quite congenial. Edward R. Butler, master of St. Louis, was "a good fellow—by nature, at first, then by profession." Doctor Albert Ames, mayor of Minneapolis, was a cheerful, kindly man, and before his downfall into personal decadence, the "best-loved" man in town. Christopher L. Magee of Pittsburgh built his machine on his "goodness of heart and personal charm." These bosses were honest about their activities and the first to admit their misdeeds. They often supplied Steffens with the very information that they knew full well he would use against them. These men were not as evil as the things they did, and Steffens was quite sure that, if the people insisted, the bosses were capable of doing much good. Despite his obvious affection for the bosses, Steffens never lost sight of the deadly threat their "system" posed to American local self-government.[16]

Traditionally, the boss had insured the election of his friends and supporters and, in return, received a share of the miscellaneous graft that came with victory. Under bosses like Butler and Magee, all this had been changed to take advantage of modern business techniques. These new bosses were businessmen not only because they acted out of self-interest. Their business genius lay also in their recognition that success in any enterprise depended on organization. They made corruption an industry. In St. Louis, "Butler organized and systematized and developed it into a regular financial institution, and made it an integral part of the business community." He arranged the members of the municipal legislature into "combines" and sold their votes. There was a regular schedule of fees for everything, and everything was put up for sale. The same was true in Pittsburgh. Magee and his allies carefully catalogued the city's resources, services, and franchises and then auctioned them off as their private property. In essence, big business and corporations demanded efficient corruption, and the bosses supplied it.[17]

The implications of this analysis were so staggering that Steffens fell over them. Without fully realizing it, he was describing a revolutionary change in American business, politics, and government. The old haphazard forms of municipal corruption were entrepreneurial; they were part of a small business, small town, commercial way of life. This would never do for a modern corporation. The age of big business demanded efficient corruption to protect enormous investments and profits. In politics and government, the bosses were providing the rationality so necessary for complex, organized capital and industry. In his *Autobiography*, Steffens remembered that, "I could hardly believe what I was seeing." He could not carry his analysis, which was so close to that of the socialist, to its logical conclusion. Instead, he turned back to a more comfortable frame of reference and rejoined the middle class.[18]

For Steffens, the bottom of society was as responsible as the top for the destruction of democratic, local government. If the rich bought corruption, the "riffraff" sold it. In St. Louis, Butler ruled with the assistance of the "worst elements of both parties." Illiterate, irresponsible, and immoral saloon keepers and other low types, "catching the smell of corruption, rushed into the Municipal Assembly, drove out the remaining respectable men, and sold the city." In Pittsburgh, Magee carefully set up his machine on the same basis, seeing to the election of "bartenders, saloon-keepers, liquor dealers and others allied with vice." Not content with their own corruption, these avaricious "creatures" of the bosses sought to ruin others for profit. In Philadelpha, the political ring protected vice, imported white slavery from New York, financed saloons, and encouraged the growth of gambling until it encompassed even school children. All this paled in comparison to the police system of graft in Minneapolis.[19]

With the good citizens of that city too busy to rule themselves, they left the task to "loafers, saloon keepers, gamblers, criminals and the thriftless poor of all types." If business boodle was high corruption, police graft was low corruption. Mayor Ames and his cohorts set out to organize all the vice in the community for their own profit. The police not only protected criminal activity, they encouraged it. They imported gamblers to set up crooked card games. They helped plan and execute robberies. The police persuaded prostitutes to set up business in every kind of establishment, including candy stores. While children bought sweets in the front, "a nefarious traffic was carried on in the rear."[20]

Yet corruption in Minneapolis was basically different from that in the other cities. Although Steffens refused to see it, business boodle and police graft were not comparable at all. The first was corporate, the second, personal. While Steffens insisted that there was a "system" of corruption in Minneapolis, he admitted that Ames was no match for the other bosses. Unlike Magee or Butler, he had little or no control over his operation. His lieutenants readily stole from him and from each other. As a result, the whole machine came crashing down within two years of its creation. In fact, Ames was the center of a method of graft reminiscent of Tammany's early days in New York. There was no system to it, and the true bosses had dismissed it as ineffective and dangerous for the organization. To recognize this distinction would have forced Steffens to give up some cherished notions about reform.[21]

What blinded Steffens was his typically American fascination with politics. When studying the workings of government, Steffens was essentially free from any preconceptions. Americans never had much government, took small interest in its operation, and cared little for the science of administration. As long as Steffens restricted his observations to this new concern for government, he could clearly see the system of it. The same was not true of politics. The American reform tradition was a political one. It was concerned with investigating and eliminating the illegitimate methods men used to win elections and gain influence in government. Americans firmly believed that the reformation of society was the task of politics, not government. They believed that politics corrupted government and seldom considered the possibility that it could be the other way around. Steffan was very much a part of this heritage. He was a genteel reformer who was rapidly becoming a progressive. Consequently, Steffens emerged from his study of municipal corruption with "two pictures, one on top of the other, on the canvas of my mind." At the same time as he described a new system of government corruption, he tenaciously held on to his old political perspective. The article on Minneapolis allowed him to combine the two. It restored familiarity to the landscape of corruption and thereby allowed Steffens to offer long-honored political solutions.[22]

Having vividly portrayed the enormous scope and depth of municipal corruption, Steffens' "cure" was a revival of personal virtue. The streets of St. Louis had crumbled into dust. The water supply was no more than "liquid mud." Despite the expenditure of millions of dollars, the city hall remained unfinished, and there was little hope that it would be completed in the near future. Municipal services and franchises were sold right out from under the citizens of Philadelphia. The St. Louis politicians thought this such a fine idea that they were going to do it themselves. According to Steffens, the answer to all this was "good conduct in the individual, simple honesty, courage and efficiency." This, Steffens assured his readers, was a more radical answer to the system of corruption than either socialism or anarchy.[23]

This, of course, was a return to the traditional equation for corruption and reform. In it, the corruption of politics caused the corruption of government. The key to the failure of local government was the boss's control of the electoral process. Using corrupt methods, the candidates of the boss gained public office. Once elected, these servants of the machine quickly succumbed to the temptations of power. Naturally, they shared their loot with their master, the boss. The solution was to wrest the electoral process from the hands of the boss and elect good men. Without political power, the boss was incapable of corrupting government. Yet, Steffens had proved this formulation to be false or, at least, very misleading. As a system, government corruption had developed into an independent source of evil, no longer completely dependent upon the control of the political process for its success. Butler's career in St. Louis was a perfect example. He began as an old-fashioned political boss who relied on his control of the electoral process for his position. Then a revolutionary change took place. In a brilliant insight, Steffens recognized that "his political influence began to depend upon his boodling instead of the reverse." Having said this, Steffens set out to describe and reform the political system.[24]

Here was a system that Steffens, reformers, and the American public well understood. Steffens developed two models of "autocracy" that permitted the bosses and their gangs to displace municipal democracy. The first was the organized majority, where the machine controlled the major political party in the city. Oftentimes, the boss dominated the second party as well. This was a useful method of disciplining any recalcitrant members of his own organization. Finally, this prevented the secondary party from combining with the reformers to overthrow the machine's rule. This was the basis for the boss's power in Pittsburgh, Philadelphia, and

Minneapolis. The second system called for a much more delicate touch by the boss. In this case, the two parties were evenly balanced, with neither being able to gain the continued allegiance of a majority of the voters. As an "unscrupulous opportunist," the boss manipulated his crucial ballots to sway the election to the candidates who paid his price. In return for victory, they agreed to do the boss's bidding in the municipal legislature. This was how Butler operated in St. Louis.[25]

Political partisanship made possible both systems of machine rule. The American voter was "herded into parties and stupefied with convictions and a name, Republican or Democrat." In a sense, Steffens' denunciation of bad citizenship was no more than a condemnation of partisan politics. It was the old genteel warning dressed up in new, dramatic language. Voting along party lines was a habitual practice of the American people and, therefore, the easy way out of public responsibility. The habit had gone so far in Philadelphia that the contented citizens of that city did not even bother to go to the polls. Staying at home, they permitted the all too willing machine to vote for them. If this trend continued, the result would be absolutism, and the only remedy, revolution. Still, Steffens had seen too much to be satisfied with the traditional prescriptions for political reform.

Steffens knew that, more often than not, these prescriptions did not work. There was a pattern to municipal reform movements, and inevitably, the result was failure. According to the "standard course," the politicians were permitted "to take over government, corrupt and deceive the people, and run things, for private profit of the boss and his ring till the corruption becomes rampant and a scandal." This was the "Tweed stage of corruption," where the stealing was bold and haphazard. Shocked by the brazen character of the thieves, the good people of the city roused themselves to throw the crooks from office. To give themselves clean government, they elected a leading businessman as mayor. While in office, he would push through the adoption of a new municipal charter and provide clean, efficient government. To the chagrin of the reformers, the boss waited and prepared for the next election and then returned to power.[26]

Steffens attributed such defeats to several factors. For one thing, reform depended too much on the "spasmodic efforts" of a fickle citizenry. Once the people returned to their normal routines and forgot politics, the way was again open for the boss and his gang to recapture the government. Yet, one of the chief aims of Steffens' articles and book was to awaken the American people to the dangers of municipal corruption. He appeared to be as guilty of the old, ineffective tactics as the reformers he so roundly criticized in his writing. There was, however, an essential difference between them. Steffens accused previous reformers of always seeking "somebody that will give us good government or something that will make it." Americans held an "ancient superstition" that democracy could somehow be made automatic and self-regulating. For Steffens, this was pure delusion.[27]

Neither an honest business administration nor a strong character could guarantee good government for long. As mayors, businessmen often proved too weak to resist the temptations of office. Their vanity and ambition made them easy prey for the seductive but empty offerings of the politicians. If they happened to be personally strong, they were not effective politicians. Mayor Seth Low of New York was a perfect example of this "bourgeois reformer type." The reformers had drawn up new municipal charters for just such men. They placed full power and responsibility for the city's management in the hands of the mayor. Under Mayor Low, New York was putting this combination to the "test." At first, the results were just what the reformers wanted from government. Mayor Low's administration was "not only honest, but able, undeniably one of the best in the whole country." He governed in such a businesslike fashion that he ruined his chances for reelection. The talents of the business executive were not those of the politician. Mayor Low was far from being a "lovable character." Because he was a model businessman, he lacked those human elements that most attracted the affection of the electorate. He was humorless and smug, obstinate and secretive. As Steffens predicted, Mayor Low and his excellent business administration were easily beaten at the polls by the Tammany machine. Again, the paradox was central to Steffens' analysis; good government inevitably led to bad government.[28]

Adding irony to paradox, Steffens showed how good government made bad government better. The bosses, not the businessmen, quickly learned the political lessons of failed reform. It was the blatant nature of corruption that caused the voters to rebel against machine rule. Understanding this, the bosses tried to put an end to the miscellaneous graft that was the source of so much public scandal. They learned to manage and centralize municipal corruption so that there was little chance of it ever reaching the light of day. The bosses were even willing to forego the profits of vice. Police graft was difficult to organize and too often horrified the good citizens of the city. If the people demanded an upstanding businessman for their mayor, this was fine with the bosses. They recognized the advantage of having such a man in office. While the machine went about the business of corruption, the honest but confused mayor gave every appearance of propriety in government.[29]

In an effort to perfect their control, the bosses were willing, even happy, to provide the community with some of the benefits of good government. The demands of the people were small. They were easily satisfied with clean water, well-paved streets, sufficient transportation, and a minimum level of public order and safety. A tacit bargain was struck between the good citizens and the machine. In return for adequate services, the public was ready to let the bosses have their way. The politicians robbed the city of millions with rakeoffs from municipal construction, contracts, and franchises. The voters only asked that all this be done quietly, without disturbing them. The community was receiving something, at least, for the tax dollars of its citizens. Unknowingly, the good government reformers had taught the bosses how to correct their mistakes and make the business of corruption more acceptable to society.

Having described the system as almost invincible and traditional reformers as fools at best, Steffens offered his final political solution. His answer to the problem of corruption was good, strong men. In the light of his own analysis, this idea appeared to be a ludicrous, even perverse, joke. Yet, Steffens seriously argued that this corrupt system that either co-opted or overwhelmed its opponents could be tamed by individuals. Superficially, the men Steffens admired and used as examples to prove his case were quite similar to the good government reformers he detested so much. With the possible exception of Joseph Folk, they were businessmen. Hovey Clarke, the courageous head of the grand jury in Minneapolis, owned a lumber company. Oliver McClintock, who fought Boss Magee in Pittsburgh, was a merchant. In Philadelphia, John Wanamaker, the tenacious enemy of that city's machine, was a corporate tycoon and millionaire. George Cole was five feet of dynamic businessman who took on the bosses in Chicago and beat them at their own game. His successor, Walter Fisher, was a corporate lawyer. To Steffens, these men were not the usual businessman-reformer or politician. They were true political leaders, and this was the difference that promised success.

It was the nature of the struggle that first attracted Steffens to these men. In St. Louis he discovered Joseph Folk, the fighting district attorney, who was investigating the Butler machine. This young lawyer was "a man at work there, one man, working all alone." The drama of a single individual standing against all the organized power of the system proved irresistible to Steffens. Folk and his campaign became a moral, political, and literary model for Steffens. Steffens saved his greatest contempt and most vitriolic prose for the righteous hypocrite who spoke of goodness but practiced evil. The very opposite was true of Folk. The proof of his character lay in his actions, not his words. Here was a man who was doing his duty, exposing corruption and prosecuting the grafters. The very unevenness of the contest gave evidence of his integrity. His only weapons were "courage and personal conviction." Aligned against him was the awesome power of organized corruption. The servants of the system, the businessmen, tried to bribe Folk with offers of riches, success, and high office. When this did not work, the bosses resorted to threats and intimidation. Still alone, Folk persisted in doing his duty with the steadfastness of the truly moral man.[30]

For all their public service, Folk, Clarke, McClintock, and the others were not representative of their communities. They were not selected by their fellow citizens to take up arms against corruption. They were not the products of popular movements. In truth, quite the contrary was true. The appointment of Clarke to the grand jury was a fortuitous "accident." The same could be said of Folk in St. Louis. The Democratic machine elected him to soothe the consciences of good citizens. No one, especially the good citizens, expected him to take his job seriously. McClintock's lonely fight in Pittsburgh was carried out at his own expense. The unexpected crusades of these men against corruption only brought out "the virtuous cowardice, the baseness of the decent citizens." McClintock's investigations were greeted with frowns, warnings, and boycotts by his fellow businessmen. Seeing the police graft exposed by Clarke and his grand jury, the leading citizens of Minneapolis did not applaud their courage and tenacity. Instead, they tried to "dissuade them from their course." The people of St. Louis "laughed" and ridiculed Folk for his apparently hopeless pursuit of Butler and his machine.[31]

Put bluntly, Steffens argued that these men succeeded, not because of democracy, but in spite of it. If they had faithfully represented their communities, they would have done nothing to stop corruption. Instead, as reflections of the public will, they would have accepted, even protected, municipal graft. Fortunately, they were not ordinary citizens but extraordinary men who towered above the masses. Because they were the exception, not the rule, they were well-prepared to fight the necessarily lonely struggle for reform. Steffens' description of Clarke was typical: "he had the habit of command, the impatient, imperious manner of the master, and the assurance of success which begets it." As "fighters," they cared little that the public either opposed them or stood idly by and watched the contest. Without support, Folk "proceeded with his work quickly, surely, smilingly, without fear or pity." They were leaders with few followers; reform generals without armies. They were what Steffens constantly looked for throughout his life—heroes.[32]

In Minneapolis, Chicago, and St. Louis, the machines were already retreating before the onslaught of this new kind of reformer. For all its strength, Steffens believed that the system of corruption had an innate flaw. In essence, the system was little more than organized immorality and, consequently, attracted weak and selfish men to its banner. The corrosive influence of corruption even destroyed its architects. Boss Butler became fat and rich, neglecting his own organization for greater personal profit. The depravity of "Doc" Ames knew no bounds as venality replaced devotion to his wife and children. When Ames' wife died, Steffens described how "the family would not have the father at the funeral, but he appeared—not at the house—but in a carriage on the street. He sat across the way, with his feet up and a cigar in his mouth, till the funeral moved; then he circled around, crossing . . . and making altogether a scene." The spirit of corruption was that of the mercenary. Recognizing no virtue except greed, the system was an empty shell. Unwilling to abide by the rules of their organization, the grafters and boodlers squabbled among themselves, cheated, and stole from each other. Without integrity and character, they were incapable of courage and loyalty.

Confronted with the righteous tenacity of Clarke and Folk, the gangs soon cracked like so many rotten melons. Under the "hard eye" of Clarke, criminals turned state's evidence to save themselves. First defiance, then consternation, and finally panic spread among the grafters. When bribery and intimidation did not work, they begged forgiveness, turned on their friends, or fled the city. Under indictment, "Boss" Ames sneaked from the city by train in the dead of night, "an unlighted cigar in his mouth, his face ashen and drawn." The story was the same in St. Louis. At first, Butler could not believe that Folk was actually after him. As Folk's purpose became clear, "terror spread and the rout was complete." The relentless prosecuting attorney sought indictments, won convictions, and slowly closed in on the heart of the machine, Butler. Still confident, Butler accepted the challenge, went to trial and, to the amazement of a skeptical public, was found guilty of bribery.[33]

Yet Steffens recognized the inherent limitations of these victories. The heroic reformers were capable of exposing and prosecuting corruption, but they could not rule without the support of the people. He asked the central question, "Is democracy possible?" The answer was still uncertain. In New York, Mayor Low's good government administration had been rejected by the voters. Philadelphia was unabashedly content to be ruled by the machine. In Pittsburgh, the reformers had been outmaneuvered by a new boss and saw triumph turned into bitter defeat. The supreme court of Missouri had overturned the convictions of the boodlers and freed "Boss" Butler. Still, there were some hopeful signs. The citizens of Minneapolis had learned their lesson and elected good men to office. Even unashamed St. Louis was showing indications of awakening to its civic duty. Most promising of all was the experiment being carried out in Chicago.[34]

For Steffens, the Chicago reformers combined the virtues of righteousness with the advantages of the system. They were both fighters and organizers, moralists and managers. Their "wrath" at the corruption of their city was no less than that of other reformers. Still, they were not satisfied with "moral fits" that temporarily washed the corrupt politicians from office only to see them return to power as the wave of voter indignation receded into complacency. Instead of further exposures of wrongdoing, they accepted "the situation just as it was—the laws, the conditions, the political circumstances, all exactly as they were." First, they sought a man to lead them and found one in George Cole. He told the truth to the public, "plain to the verge of brutality, forcible to the limit of language, and honest to utter ruthlessness." This fighting businessman provided the publicity to get their cause before the people. Unlike other reformers, this was only their initial step.[35]

Being practical men, not theorists, these reformers had no choice but to fight the machine on its own political grounds. To do this, they "deliberately and systematically" adopted the tactics of their foe. They were more interested in the victory of their cause than the purity of their methods. They formed a "reform ring" and chose their own boss. As a ring, they held mass meetings, dickered with ward heelers, traded votes, and won. Walter Fisher, the reform boss, was the archetype of this new kind of reformer: "a politician—with the education, associations, and idealism of the reformers who fail, this man has cunning, courage, tact, and rarer still, faith in the people. In short, reform in Chicago has such a leader as corruption alone usually has; a first-class executive mind and a natural manager of men." In Chicago, the hero and the boss had been made one. Publicity had aroused the people, and organization and leadership had forged them into an effective instrument of reform.[36]

The Shame of the Cities, especially the article on Chicago, reveals Steffens to be a pragmatist. As a way of seeing social reality, pragmatism is a scientific, experimental method of inquiry into the nature of human experience. As a way of acting, it is the application of profound moral and ethical concerns to that scientifically defined experience of society. *The Shame of the Cities* is an investigation of the American experience of municipal politics, government mismanagement, and reform. Steffens carefully catalogued and typed what he found: "St. Louis exemplified boodle; Minneapolis, police graft; Pittsburgh, a political and industrial machine; and Philadelphia, general civic corruption; so Chicago was an illustration of reform, and New York of good government." When Steffens argued that his method was unscientific, he was only admitting that it was not value free. He never pretended that his articles were without purpose. Steffens passionately wanted to see the restoration of democratic, representative government to the American city.[37]

His analysis of reform movements in New York and Chicago perfectly characterizes his pragmatic combination of scientific method with moral purpose. Under Mayor Low, New York had embarked on the often-tried effort of achieving reform through good government by businessmen. Thirty years of experience showed this to be the "wrong road—crowded with unhappy American cities." This was not an experiment, but a tragically stubborn habit that could only lead to failure. On the other hand, the Chicago reformers were true pragmatists. They refused to repeat the mistakes of the past. Experimenting, they sought new ways of accomplishing reform and soon found success using the methods of their enemy, the machine. These reformers, unlike their counter-

parts in New York, realized that the tactics of the boss were not syn-
onymous with his corrupt ends. The value of the tools of practical
politics lay in their purpose, not their use. Consequently, these
reformers "broke many a cherished reform principle, but few rules
of practical politics." As a result, they were freeing Chicago by
means of a democratic system ruled by a reform boss. For the next
eight years, Steffens would continue to use himself and his journalism as tools in this long struggle for representative government.[38]

CHAPTER 4

In and Out of the Muck

T HE January 1903 issue of *McClure's Magazine* was a landmark in the development of muckraking. Besides Steffens' article on Minneapolis, the publication also offered its readers a chapter of Ida Tarbell's *History of the Standard Oil Company* and Ray Stannard Baker's "The Right to Work: The Story of the Non-Striking Miners." The former explored the rise of John D. Rockefeller to absolute control of the oil industry; the latter described the suffering of nonunion laborers during the anthracite coal strike in Pennsylvania. In his editorial, McClure found the common theme that linked together the three articles. They showed "capitalists, workingmen, politicians, citizens—all breaking the law." If this "dangerous trait" continued to grow, McClure warned, there would be no one left to defend the law. The final cost would be no less than "the sum total . . . of our liberty." These words signaled the rise of muckraking and progressivism to national consciousness.[1]

Muckraking expressed the profound middle class concern with the growing power of social, political, and economic combinations in all phases of American life. In business and industry, the trust and the corporation had replaced the entrepreneur as the model for enterprise. Workingmen were no longer independent craftsmen but laborers and unskilled workers organizing themselves into unions. Fewer and fewer Americans lived in small communities where leadership was a reward for family ties or personal accomplishment. Instead, the future lay in large urban centers that depended on a complex system of services and bureaucratic structures for their very existence. In politics, the middle class found its voice being overwhelmed by the power of organized groups and interests. In the dim first light of the new century, the muckrakers brought the harsh reality of this urban, industrial world home to their readers in the clear sharpness of print.

To do this, the muckrakers used the methods of the infant social

56

sciences. College educated, the muckrakers at *McClure's* meticulously researched their subjects and provided full documentation for their findings. At *McClure's* at least, there was to be no mistaking fact for fiction. In this sense, the muckrakers were no more than sophisticated reporters of the world around them. They were describing in coherent terms the social, economic, and political conditions of emerging, modern America. Steffens was well suited for this task. Trained in experimental psychology at European universities, he knew how to gather and arrange evidence systematically. Yet, the muckrakers were more than investigative journalists with the talents of amateur historians, sociologists, and political scientists. As with Steffens, they reported the facts in order to destroy them.

The muckrakers shared a deep suspicion of two apparently contradictory trends in American life. At first glance, society appeared to be fragmenting in the face of the catastrophic unheavals of the late nineteenth century. Depression, strikes, violence, political turmoil, and class warfare threatened the basic unity of society that was so dear to the middle class. Strangely, this process did not lead to chaos, but to the rise of "interests" made up of segments of this once unified society. This gave birth to a shift in individual allegiance from the community, whether it be local, state, or national, to these new, specialized organizations. The threat to American democracy was clear. In a broader context than McClure's editorial, the muckrakers asked: If no one concerned themselves with the good of society, who would care for the interests of the community? The enemy was all those who joined together to further their own profit, power, and privilege at the expense of the people.

The reaction of the muckrakers to all this was one of "righteous indignation." They did not write of their discoveries in the disinterested manner of scientists but with the intensity of the moralists. These "systems," "invisible governments," and "special interests" were corrupting and undermining the moral base of the nation, democratic government. In hundreds of articles, they exposed what they saw as efforts by the trusts, unions, and political machines to thwart the will of the people. Yet the muckrakers did not consider their revelations to be reason for despair. They had a naive, almost mystical faith in the goodness of the American people. Given their reverence for the righteousness of the citizenry, the muckrakers were sure that these sinister powers of selfishness could only flourish in the darkness of secrecy. Once exposed by the muckrakers for all to see, the contest would clearly become one between "the interests" and the "people." Such a struggle could only end with the triumph of the public will and the restoration of American democracy.[2]

Steffens' enthusiasm for reform was typical of the muckrakers. He was as sure as any of his colleagues that their work would lead to the reformation of society. Steffens deeply resented the suggestion that *The Shame of the Cities* made him a prophet of municipal doom. He found it disturbing that any reader would interpret his articles as being "pessimistic." Beneath all the descriptions of graft and corruption, he told his father, "there is the assumption that something can be done and that men are willing to do it." Steffens and the other muckrakers did not have to look far for proof. All over the United States, reformers were rising to power in municipal government and challenging the "system" of corruption. In the White House, Theodore Roosevelt was preaching reform and using his "big stick" to whip the trusts into line. These were the first signs of a stirring reform movement that would sweep the nation.[3]

Yet, in one very important respect, Steffens was not a typical muckraker. He had a greater personal stake in the success of investigative journalism than most of the other writers at *McClure's*. Ida Tarbell, the grande dame of muckraking, was already a competent and successful author of popular history. The young Ray Stannard Baker saw himself as a novelist. Muckraking was only to be a temporary diversion for him. The role of the historian was too passive for Steffens. He was not satisfied to recount the heroics of others but, if possible, wanted to help shape the course of events. Steffens had already tried his hand at writing a novel, and the result had been a dismal failure. Of all the muckrakers, Steffens was most surely the journalist, and he fully recognized that his fate as a writer lay in that profession. He could not afford to be caught up in a failure. Such a disaster could well destroy his career.

For Steffens, muckraking was a test of his art, his profession, and even his worth as a man. Consequently, the success of his series on municipal corruption was a deeply satisfying, personal triumph for him. With almost boyish glee, he told his mother that "these are happy days for me, laborious; but the work wins, so who minds?" The popular and critical acclaim received by his articles and book made his name as a national journalist. He reported to his father that "*The Shame of the Cities* is actually selling. It is being reviewed everywhere and together with the last article, is making quite a stir. Maybe I'll beat some of the novels." Such recognition was proof that journalism was as much art as any other form of writing, especially the one he had tried and failed to master.[4]

At the same time, muckraking was a trial for his manhood. Steffens was daring, even foolhardy, in the pursuit of evidence and information for his articles. In Minneapolis, he boldly confronted two dangerous criminals in order to verify the authenticity of the "Big Mit" ledger. Yet, according to his *Autobiography*, Steffens still felt himself a fraud. He had done no original research in either St. Louis or Minneapolis. Instead, "I had simply gone where some one else, Joe Folk or Hovey Clarke, had been doing the work, and picking up the fruits of their labor and risk." In short, Steffens thought himself guilty of watching life, not living it. He had to convince himself that he was as worthy as Folk or Clarke of meeting the challenge of the "system." So, with "dread," Steffens went "alone" to Pittsburgh to "investigate and expose the corruption of that invisible government which looked so big and strong, so menacing and—so invisible." Steffens emerged from this test in "hell" with his confidence as a man and his story as a journalist. The two were inseparable for Steffens.[5]

To this point in his career, Steffens had never been able to distinguish his ambition from either his art or the social purpose of his writing. It was for this reason that his wife's exposure of his own "righteousness" so profoundly shook Steffens. When two articles on labor corruption by Ray Stannard Baker appeared in *McClure's* and overshadowed Steffens' own accounts of state mismanagement, Josephine severely chided her husband for giving away his ideas. Steffens had originally discovered the basis for Baker's articles in Chicago. Instead of waiting and eventually writing the stories himself, Steffens recommended Baker for the job. Steffens protested to his wife that he was positive that his young colleague would give him full credit for his contribution. In any event, Steffens argued, the important thing was not the author but the getting of the truth to the American people.

At loggerheads, they invited Baker to dinner to find out who was right about the matter. When it turned out that their guest had no memory of the true origin of the articles, Josephine smiled in triumph. Steffens was stunned by his own reaction to the episode. He was completely humiliated to have been proven so wrong by his wife. Obviously, she knew more about his motives and ambitions than Steffens himself. Moreover, he was not at all happy for his friend Baker. Instead, he was mean with envy that Baker should accomplish so much with Steffens' idea and then not give him any recognition. Steffens was aghast at this evidence of his own weaknesses and egotism. He forced himself to recognize that he was no better than the businessmen and good citizens that he so easily condemned in his writings.[6]

If Pittsburgh had been his "hell," then a "long, lone railroad journey" soon after this incident became his Gethsemane. Shutting himself up in his compartment, he set out to face his "yellow streak" and prove his own selfishness. Finding the "yellow" in his character was the easy part. Steffens quickly recognized that he was as guilty of such petty emotions as jealousy and envy as any other man. Seeing himself a hypocrite and a crook was a much more difficult task. As he related it in his *Autobiography:*

I didn't want to be righteous, and there I was, exactly like the righteous who were corrupted by their own ignorance of their own graft. How did I differ from them? They also thought they were not bribed; and they didn't do anything felonious. But they were slowed up as reformers and voters by—what? By their business interest. They were not bought by the briber's money; they were bribed by their own money. And—so was I. Nobody could, by an offer of money make me suppress a fact or color a truth, but—yes, I did go a bit slow—sometimes—in something I wrote. Why? To keep my job, to keep my credit, to hold my readers and "get by" my editors. Well, that was it. I was cheap, like any other good man; I did not come high like an honest crook; I could be "got" by my own salary. And the psychology of that was the psychology of the bribe-taker, whether the bribe-taker knew he was a bribe-taker or thought he was an honest man.

Armed with this intelligence, Steffens would never again mistake himself for a good man. He would no longer be a "cynic or a fool" about his own virtues or those of others.[7]

This discovery of his own corruption made him even less critical of the wrongdoing of other men. He believed that few men, including himself, had the character to escape the pernicious influence of the "system." Consequently, the humbled journalist sympathized with the plight of both the rulers and the servants of organized evil. In his view, all men, whether they be bosses, heelers, or businessmen, were victims of systematic corruption. For Steffens, the "system" was the social and political equivalent of original sin. This new appreciation of the pervasive power of corruption only deepened his suspicion of self-proclaimed good men. While the bosses were as aware of their failings as Steffens, these self-serving hypocrites were either fools or the unwitting tools of the "system." A man with the audacity to pronounce himself free of the taint of corruption must be either a saint or a simpleton. Steffens knew few of the former but many of the latter. As a result, he reserved much of his affection and respect for the bosses and his greatest skepticism for the reformers.

In his short story, "The Honesty of Honest Tom," Steffens explored this difference between the truthful bad man and the self-deceiving honest man. Thomas Harding, a genial political boss, and Elisha Leyman, a wealthy wholesaler and reformer, are both attending a meeting of the board of directors of a large company. When the annual business of the bribe for the state treasurer comes before the board, Leyman rises to leave the room. Harding calls him back and demands an explanation. In the confrontation that ensues between the two, the good reformer accuses the boss of being a "crook and a grafter." "Honest Tom" freely admits his guilt, but accuses Leyman of the same crimes and worse. The boss challenges the merchant to end this particular bit of graft by voting against the bribe. If he will do that, Harding will use all his power and influence in the general fight against corruption. It is obvious to everyone in the meeting that the boss really wants to join the struggle for reform. When the role is called, the crestfallen and for once honest good man can only raise his hand in support of the bribe.[8]

Steffens always remembered the moral of his own tale in his interviews with bosses and masters of the "system." Bold in approach but gentle in judgment, Steffens was a brilliant interviewer. He credited his subjects with intelligence and the honesty that he felt went with it. At the same time, Steffens never presented himself as being in any way superior to these organizers of corruption. As he was fond of saying, the bosses recognized that "I was one of them." His questions were sharp and pointed—those of a man who wanted the truth and knew where and how to get it. If the interviewees began to make self-serving speeches, Steffens would immediately pull them up short. He was questioning them to gain knowledge, not to hear propaganda. Like them, Steffens was a man of the world and did not expect to be treated as a fool. Fascinated by his reputation and comforted by his understanding, the bosses willingly granted Steffens his interviews. At times, they even sought him out to tell him and the nation their side of the story.[9]

The results were intriguing descriptions of personal power and human frailty. There was Frederick Weyerhauser, the lumber king, who could neither calculate the enormity of his fortune nor the painful, personal cost of building it with unsavory business practices. In Cincinnati, Steffens sought out George Cox, the gruff, old tyrant of the Queen City. Well past his prime, but still haughty and proud, Cox wanted to impress the investigating journalist with the excellence of his machine. When Steffens judged Cox's organization to be only "pretty good," the disgusted boss retorted, " 'best you ever saw.' " Steffens was especially fond of Israel Durham, boss of Philadelphia. When Steffens was in the City of Brotherly Love, Durham would sneak up to his hotel room, and the two would debate urban politics and corruption with the skill of "scientists." Steffens saw Durham, like so many of his kind, as a trapped victim of the "system." While admitting the evil of his machine, Durham plaintively asked Steffens, " 'Just what do I do that's so rotten wrong?' " Realizing that the boss was very ill, Steffens refused to answer the question. Called to the bed of the dying boss, Steffens finally told Durham the nature of his crime. He, Steffens explained, was a "born leader of the common man," and he had betrayed their trust to "rich business men and other enemies of the people." Durham was a "traitor to his own." The boss took this brutal truth "straight," with understanding and courage. For all his appreciation of the bosses as men, Steffens never confused his sympathy for them with admiration for their cause.[10]

Steffens was a reformer and a progressive. There was no mistaking this. His affection for the bosses was tempered by his hatred of their machines. His personal skepticism about good men was checked by the success of progressive reform. Steffens was a man of his times, and he imbibed all the passion and enthusiasm of his era. His career as a muckraker paralleled the rise of progressivism to the national scene. As early as the 1890s, Hazen Pingree in Detroit and a host of urban reformers in Wisconsin had begun to challenge the forces of corruption in their cities. Steffens' *The Shame of the Cities* was published near the height of urban reform. Samuel "Golden Rule" Jones was applying his peculiar mixture of Christianity and socialism to the governing of Toledo, Ohio. Folk was cleaning up St. Louis. The man who gave Steffens the most hope was Mayor Tom Johnson of Cleveland.

As a man, a politician, and a leader, Johnson had every trait admired by Steffens. He was "efficient like Fisher, forceful and energetic like Roosevelt, and honest and persistent like Joe Folk." Beyond all this, his greatest virtue was his "intellectual integrity." Johnson was not a naive good man, but a practical businessman who had made millions buying, selling, and manipulating streetcar franchises. In short, he had spent much of his life as a corrupter of municipal government. At the height of his career, he was converted to reform by Henry George's writings. Because he had been a sinner himself, Johnson knew how the "system" operated and why "privilege" ruined the best of men. This "intelligence" enabled Johnson to lead the people of Cleveland to true reform and representative government. Through speeches, public meetings, and debates, Johnson gained the confidence of the people. With their support, he proposed and won basic tax reforms for the city. Under his guidance, the city provided excellent police protection and services for its citizens. His administration attracted young idealists who thought "it can be a joy to serve one's city." The awed Steffens announced to the world that "Tom Johnson is the best Mayor of the best-governed city in the United States." [11]

Almost as soon as Steffens had found this most perfect of urban reformers, progressivism moved to the state level, and Steffens moved with it. Beginning in April 1904, Steffens published his series, "Enemies of the Republic," in *McClure's*. Later published in book form as *The Struggle for Self-Government*, it explores the corruption of state politics. He dedicated the book to Nicholas II, czar of Russia. With heavy-handed irony, Steffens explained to the monarch that he need not fear granting his people representative government. As practiced in the United States, this form of government posed no threat to absolute rule. Although they claimed differently, Americans neither "understood self- or representative government" nor did they "demand it." In a classic formulation of the progressive creed, Steffens argued that "our representative democracy represents not the people, but the protected business of a few of the people, and protected business is—privilege." To be fair, Steffens warned the czar that there were some "signs of the dawn of political intelligence here and there now and then." In essence, the "Dedication" was little more than a repetition of the "Introduction" to *The Shame of the Cities*. [12]

The articles were no less severe in tone. In his investigation of municipal corruption, Steffens found that "the stream of pollution branched off in the most unexpected directions and spread out in a network of arteries so complex that hardly any part of the body politic seemed clear of it." With what was becoming an old refrain, Steffens saw corruption as not only "political, but financial and industrial, too." In an effort to find its heart, Steffens pursued the "throbbing arteries" of corruption through state government to big business and even into the United States Senate. There sat Senator Nelson Aldrich of Rhode Island, the leader of the Republican party in that chamber and, for some, " 'the boss of the United States.' " According to Steffens, Aldrich was an "inordinately selfish man," who represented the greediest corporate interest in the country. Here must be the end of the line of corruption. In fact, it was not.[13]

Steffens' analysis was not linear but circular. The line of corruption began with the American people and ended with them. Like so many progressives, Steffens was caught in his profound belief in the people. Unlike them, Steffens was willing to carry this article of democratic faith to its logical conclusion. If the people were the ultimate source of representative self-government, then they also must be responsible for its demise. Consequently, Steffens insisted that Aldrich represented not only the corporations but also "the rest of us, and that is the matter with us." Americans were not acting as a people defending the common good, but as individuals concerned with their own selfish interests. There would be no end to the "system" until "reform begins at home—with all of us."

Not every article in the series was so bleak, and as Steffens had warned the czar, there were some "signs" of the awakening of the people. In "Wisconsin: Representative Government Restored," Steffens gave his readers a real hero, Governor Robert LaFollette. When he first heard of LaFollette, Steffens, always skeptical of good men, was sure that the young governor must be "a charlatan and a crook." He went to Wisconsin to investigate and expose this "demagogue." To his surprise, Steffens discovered "the story of the heroism it takes to fight in America for American ideals." His praise of LaFollette was of the same kind that he lavished on Mayor Johnson. Here was no "white-robed, spotless angel" but an ambitious, practical politician "who wants to serve the people." First, this charismatic leader aroused the citizens of his state with his fiery oratory and carefully reasoned arguments.Then, LaFollette organized the people into an effective political machine to combat the systematic corruption of their government. The result was "honest, reasonable, intelligent citizenship" and victory for both the people and LaFollette.[14]

"Enemies of the Republic" was both not enough and too much for President Theodore Roosevelt. He confided to McClure that Steffens should "put more sky in the landscape." For Roosevelt, there was entirely too much emphasis on business crime and political corruption in his friend's articles. The president's complaint reflected his growing discomfort with the journalism of exposé. Encouraged by their popularity, Steffens and his colleagues grew ever bolder in their accusations and more virulent in their condemnation of business and political conservatives. Early in 1906, Roosevelt tried to rein in what he now considered a dangerous and destructive force in American politics and life. In two speeches, he compared the investigative reporter to the man with the muck-rake in John Bunyan's *The Pilgrim's Progress*. While admitting that the dirt needed to be "scraped up with the muck-rake," Roosevelt accused the muckraking journalist of only "seeing what is vile and debasing" and never what was "good in the world." In this manner, the muckraker distorted social reality and did a disservice to the society. With these attacks, the president coined the term "muckraker" and dealt that movement a near fatal blow.[15]

To the chagrin of the muckrakers, Roosevelt's speeches received a generally favorable response from the public. His attack revealed a serious contradiction in the nature of investigative journalism. As Steffens and his colleagues saw it, the task of the muckraker was to expose corruption and public wrongdoing. They were dedicated to bringing the hidden and secret evils of politics and society to the attention of the nation. The muckrakers succeeded and caused great excitement, consternation, and concern. Their readers certainly appreciated the vital and necessary public service being performed by the muckrakers. Nevertheless, the nation soon began to tire of this steady diet of muckraking articles and books. This was not simply the response of a fickle public. By the time of Roosevelt's speeches, it was apparent that the muckrakers had to seek out corruption. As investigative reporters, they needed the existence of human failings for their work. Their profession was to find the dark clouds in the blue of the sky. The "filth on the floor" was their business, and the muck-rake their pen.

Roosevelt's criticism of the muckrakers was more than an expression of growing public sentiment. It was also a carefully calculated defense of his own political position. The muckrakers were as much reformers as they were journalists. As such, they threatened to usurp the president's place as the symbol and voice of progressivism for the nation. The even more militant muckrakers were raising demands for reform faster than Roosevelt could ever hope to satisfy them. As publicists, they were bringing to the attention of the nation all kinds of political challengers to Roosevelt and his party. To the president's dismay, Steffens did this superbly in "Enemies of the Republic." In his article on Missouri, he supported Folk, a Democrat, for governor. LaFollette distributed thousands of copies of "Wisconsin: Representative Government Restored" in his successful bid for reelection as governor. LaFollette was now in the Senate, a rival of Roosevelt for the affection of Republican progressives. There was little wonder that Roosevelt saw these erstwhile allies in the cause of reform as his enemies.

In fact, neither the president's tirades nor public opinion were responsible for the decline of muckraking. Partly, the muckrakers themselves put an end to the need for their services. The voters heard their prophetic words and heeded their call for reform. Measuring the nation's political pulse in late 1905, Steffens declared that "the beginnings had been made toward the restoration of representative government in all the land." By 1906, the tide of progressivism had risen from the cities to the states and had begun to spill over into the Congress of the United States. Governors, senators, and representatives took over the duties of the muckrakers. From their political pulpits, they thundered forth their condemnation of the "interests," "the system," and "privilege." Within four years, the progressive movement would be the most potent force in American politics, and muckraking, while still important, would be losing its grip on the public's imagination. [16]

From the outset, Steffens was ready to join this crusade. His skepticism, which was never as deep as his writing suggested, dissolved into a hearty enthusiasm. Splitting with McClure over business, artistic, and ideological differences, Steffens resigned from the magazine. With Tarbell, Baker, and several other prominent muckrakers, he purchased *The American Magazine*. The new owners promised their readers that the journal would "reflect a happy, struggling, fighting world, in which, we believe, good people are coming out on top." Steffens wanted to make the magazine a platform for progressive candidates and issues. When his colleagues resisted his efforts to turn the journal into a propaganda organ, Steffens sold his shares in the enterprise. For the first time since his arrival in New York, Steffens was his own man, and he was ready to put muckraking behind him. [17]

Muckraking had provided Steffens with great personal rewards. As the recognized leader of that movement, Steffens had become more than a popular journalist; he was a national celebrity. His articles, speeches, even his travels were the focus of intense public interest. Still, there were drawbacks to being a muckraker. As an expositor of corruption, Steffens was little more than an acute and outraged observer of men and events. For all his popularity, he was still an outsider. Fame alone was never enough for Steffens. Psychologically, Steffens needed to be at what he considered the center of action. As a national personality, Steffens had a certain amount of influence, and he wanted to turn it into power. Becoming an advocate of reform gave him that opportunity. A good word from him was worth thousands of votes for progressive candidates. Although his relationship with Roosevelt cooled perceptibly after 1906, Steffens counted a new host of powerful political figures who asked his council and support. Tom Johnson, LaFollette, Folk, and numerous other progressive leaders called him friend. Steffens gave his energy and his art to their cause, his cause.

In small part, Steffens supported progressivism by explaining and defending its methods and goals. As always, the criteria "for public conduct must be loyalty to the common good." To further this end, Steffens advocated such progressive measures as the referendum, the popular election of senators, and the selection of candidates by primaries. Mostly, though, these articles were little more than a series of platitudes on how good citizens should fulfill their political obligations. Such essays as "Advice to the First Voter" and "Watch Your Congressman" were close to parodies of text books on civic responsibility. He told young voters that "ballots" were the "bullets" of representative democracy. They should vote for the best man regardless of his party. It was the duty of every citizen to scrutinize the record of his congressional representative. The "best source" for doing this was the *Congressional Record*. These pedestrian and lifeless articles made it apparent that Steffens had little interest in the mechanics of self-government. His faith was in men, not methods. [18]

His profiles and interviews with progressive leaders were full of vitality and insights. In *The Shame of the Cities*, Steffens lamented that "The people are sound but without leaders." Now, near the height of the progressive movement, the people could choose from a plethora of leaders of all types and persuasions. Although he was retiring from office, Theodore Roosevelt still represented the mainstream of reform. While larger than life, Roosevelt was typically American in his virtues and failings. As "elemental man in the full glory of health and strength, and courage, morally applied," the president symbolized the character of the nation. If his strength was his willingness to go "right on fighting evils wherever they showed a head," his weakness was his blindness to "the systemized Evil which lay under the superficial evils." Consequently, the "square deal" was a "very limited remedy" that did not attack the root of American corruption. Still, Steffens praised the president for locating the enemy and reasserting the sovereignty of the people over the "interests." In Steffens' judgment, "Theodore Roosevelt will go down through history as a great democratic leader rather than a great President."[19]

At the other extreme was the inscrutable William Randolph Hearst. Millionaire, newspaper baron, prolabor agitator, Hearst was running for governor of New York on an independent ticket in 1906. After a long interview with him on a train from Chicago to New York, Steffens wrote "Hearst, The Man of Mystery" for *American Magazine*. In Hearst, Steffens first glimpsed the kind of totalitarian personality that would cause so much horror and anguish in this century. In appraising his subject, Steffens recognized that "his very ability seems to be that of will, rather than mind." Intellectually, Hearst cared little for economic theory, and his understanding of the "system" was shallow at best. Still, he was willing to stir up "class hatred" to gain support and votes in his campaign. Hearst's commitment was to himself, not to ideas.[20]

As a leader, Hearst was a demagogue, not a democrat. Although Hearst did not feel its emotional "fervor," his ambition was "to personify the modern Democratic movement." Steffens realized that Hearst was "distinctly unmoral" in his will to power. Where the national reform movement was "at bottom, moral, Mr. Hearst is political." With absolute "ruthlessness," Hearst was willing to use "hate" to gain support. Unlike Roosevelt, he never could be the "representative of the spirit of the people." According to Steffens, Hearst neither had the character nor the inclination to be the instrument of the great crusade for reform: he only wanted the nation to follow him. He had the "moral sense" of the autocrat whose exercise of authority would reflect his own volition and not the voice of the people. Hearst was a "movement of his own, willing to grant the American people plutocratic government."[21]

Despite his distaste for his methods and goals, Steffens was both fascinated and perplexed by the man. If, as Oliver Wendell Holmes described him, Roosevelt was "pure act," Hearst was pure will. In his article, Steffens could not hide his admiration for a man who believed that "he might by work, intelligence and will force himself into any office in the country." Hearst presented Steffens with a bewildering problem. Like many progressives, Steffens believed that strong leaders were the solution to corruption. There was no denying that Hearst was "courageous to the degree of boldness." Moreover, he was dedicated to reform. This should have placed Hearst in the forefront of the effort to restore representative democracy. Yet, as told in his *Autobiography*, Steffens found a leader with "no moral illusions," whose purpose was "to establish some measure of democracy, with patient but ruthless—force." At this point in his life, Steffens refused to acknowledge the possible consequences of a figure such as Hearst. Steffens could not yet understand "what part a dictatorship has to play in democracy." For the moment, Hearst would have to remain "A Man of Mystery."[22]

Steffens was much more comfortable with Eugene Debs, the leader of the Socialist party in the United States. Even before the publication of his interview with Debs in the October 1903 issue of *Everybody's Magazine*, Steffens declared to his sister that, "as for socialism, I certainly am socialistic but I'm not a Socialist." In the article, Steffens made it appear as if this was his first inquiry into Marxist doctrine. He warned that American leaders must recognize and confront the "one great common problem" of American society or lose out to such "radicals" as the Socialists. As described by the sympathetic Steffens, socialism was certainly the most mild-mannered of radical solutions. "For Socialism seems to be a science. It is an interpretation of history; a theory of the evolution of society; no mere man-dreamed Utopia, as I have thought, but a faith, a calculation that, since the economic forces which have brought man from slavery up to the present state of civilization are continuous, we can foresee the next inevitable step." In a series of only superficially difficult questions that followed this statement, Steffens gave Debs the opportunity to present his views simply and coherently.[23]

While much of the article was little more than a mild propaganda piece for socialism, Steffens was more interested in the leader than his program. For Steffens, Debs was the "kindest, foolishest, most courageous lover of man in the world." It was for this reason, and not for his doctrine, that half the world hated him. Yet, Debs "loves mankind too much to be hurt of man." This was what made him so "dangerous" to the "system." He put the happiness and welfare of the people above all other considerations, whether it be "business, prosperity, property." In the final analysis, Steffens believed more in men than in their programs. Given his choice between a Debs and a Hearst, Steffens chose the man of good will over the man of iron will. This was the basis for Steffens' great personal effort to turn the tide for reform.[24]

CHAPTER 5

Christian Men

F OR all his faith in the role of great men in reform, Steffens was a firm believer in democracy. He was well aware that progressivism's dependence on strong leaders could be the movement's fatal flaw. No matter how good the leadership, a democratic movement could not succeed without popular support. Only a highly developed, national political consciousness could hope to sustain the momentum of true reform. To achieve this end, Steffens undertook the prophetic task of helping "to bring about an essential change in the American mind."[1] In *Upbuilders*, published in 1909, Steffens tried to develop this necessary interrelationship between leadership roles and civic consciousness in American democracy. The result is a brilliant, but unappreciated, effort to combine traditional moral perspectives with modern social and political analysis.

Steffens dedicated *Upbuilders* to his father; this said much about the purpose of the book. In genteel, middle class, familial culture, the father was the model for the son. By this dedication, Steffens was proudly announcing himself a fit successor to his father. Very much the same process took place in American society. Without the authority of traditional hierarchical order or the limitations of a strict class structure, American society sought models for social and political conduct in past and present heroes. By their lives, such men as Jefferson, Washington, and, especially, Lincoln set standards for behavior in a democracy. Men measured their actions by these exemplars. In *Upbuilders*, Steffens used this same method in the cause of reform. He gave the nation five leaders who should serve as "the inspiration of humble examples, and some notion of how to proceed." Their lives, actions, and beliefs offered "*the solution of our common problem; the problem of the cities, states, and nations—the problem of civilized living in human communities.*"[2]

Steffens chose the five heroes of his book with great care. He wanted to make it clear that "it has not mattered much who the leader was, or what. His religion has made no difference, nor his social status; nor his financial condition; nor his party." Mark Fagan, mayor of Jersey City, was a Catholic and a Republican. Ben Lindsey, the innovative juvenile court judge from Denver, was a Democrat and a Protestant. Most of all, Steffens was sure that class distinctions were no criteria for judging a leader. Fagan was from a poor, working class background. Everett Colby, state senator in the New Jersey legislature, was an American aristocrat by birth, a Wall Street broker by profession, and a millionaire by inheritance. Lindsey's Southern, middle class family was left destitute by the Civil War and moved to the West to recover its fortunes. Rudolph Spreckels, the San Francisco reformer, was a rich, aggressive businessman, the progeny of an already wealthy family. At the other extreme was William S. U'Ren. The father of initiative and recall was a blacksmith like his father before him. Despite the differences in status and wealth, these leaders were all *"brave, loyal, and sometimes in tears . . . serving their fellow-men."*[3]

For Steffens, class distinctions were as dangerous to democracy and reform as the "interests." He made the reason clear in the "Preface" to *Upbuilders.* According to Steffens, there were "not many educated individuals . . . as wise as the mass of men." This was true because, "though each individual in the great crowd lacks some virtues, they all together have what no individual has, a combination of all the virtues." When the people expressed their voices collectively instead of individually in a democracy, they supported the good of the nation over their personal, selfish desires. In short, the whole was greater than the sum of the parts. Representative government was a "living organism" that harmonized all the constituent segments of society. If class interests or leaders dominated politics, then the welfare of the body politic would give way to warfare among the competing classes. By their very diversity, these five leaders reflected the unity of the people and the nation. Steffens was willing to raise this expression of solidarity to the level of the divine. These men were ready to "both be and obey the voice of humanity. And that is divinity enough for Man, and for the little leaders of men."[4]

If the description of the people and their relationship to their leaders was almost mystical in language, the story of each reform leader is, in good part, religious in tone. *Upbuilders* is Steffens' attempt to adapt Christian ethics to contemporary social and political reality. He believed that reform could come only from a combination of "intelligence" and morality. "Intelligence" came first. No matter how well meaning a man might be, he could never effectively fight the "grand system" without first fully understanding it. To comprehend the nature of the "system," a man must experience it. Steffens made the tale of each reformer a parable of this journey through experience to understanding. All were like Mark Fagan, "who by following the facts, without a theory of reform, by tackling each obstacle as he approached it, came upon the truth. . . ." This discovery of the true character of corruption did not come in a flash of insight, but at the end of a long, tedious process of study and analysis of one's world. For Steffens, "intelligence" was not intuitive, but scientific. It was only after "seeing things separately with his eyes" that the reformer "came to see them together with his mind."[5]

In spite of his protestations to the contrary, Steffens made certain invidious distinctions between wealthy leaders and those from less fortunate circumstances. According to Steffens, the reformers from poorer backgrounds had a natural advantage over their rich counterparts in this struggle for understanding. Because of poverty, Mayor Fagan and Judge Lindsey were both "victims" of the "system" as children. From this experience, Fagan gained a ready affection for those who "suffered greatly from the wrongs of others." As a boy, Lindsey had to work at three jobs to help support his family. Under this burden, "he sunk . . . to the verge of despair; and he learned the value of a kind word of sympathy and good cheer." What was true of these two leaders was equally true of the "pauperized or over-worked" people. Although his definition of the people appeared all-inclusive, Steffens believed that the poorer classes were "the first, last, and best appeal in all great human cases." The reason was "not that the people are better than their betters, but that they are more disinterested; they are not possessed by possessions; they have not so many 'things' and 'friends' . . . they are free and fair." For Steffens, reform was almost a natural, inevitable act for the less fortunate classes and their leaders.[6]

The wealthy had a much more difficult time appreciating the harmful effects of the "system." Yet, according to Steffens, it could be done, and Everett Colby was proof of "what a rich young man may do if he rises above his class." As a child, he was taught only to "play" and knew none of the necessity of "work." Like so many of his kind who "cannot learn," he was ill-equipped to understand the world around him. All life was a game, and he was an avid player. Colby entered politics only for the "excitement" of the contest. Still, his "instincts" were good, and he slowly realized that the "privileges" he enjoyed from birth were the products of "corrupted government." Colby lost his "class consciousness" and joined the effort to reform the "grosser vices of his own class." At this point, Steffens drew back from the implications of this comparison between Colby and Lindsey or Fagan. It was not just upper class consciousness that was destructive to the common good but any kind of class politics. For Steffens, the foundation for reform was spiritual, not economic.[7]

Steffens was aiming at Christ, not Marx. The answer to corruption was not "class-conscious folly" but a change in the heart. "Intelligence" was the prerequisite step, but only a step, to the political equivalent of the religious conversion experience. Steffens was familiar with this transformation in personal consciousness; he had experienced it himself on the train after his wife had exposed his own failings. "Intelligence" was no more than the dawning self-awareness of one's selfish passions in a society corrupted by the "system." This understanding in the mind led to a change in social perspective. A person who appreciated his own weaknesses could never condemn others for succumbing to temptation. This was as much as Steffens was willing to claim for himself at the moment. He credited the reform leaders with much more. Steffens believed that man had a natural, emotional disposition to do good. When "intelligence" swept away the ignorance of personal and social evil, this generous impulse then moved these leaders to embrace their fellow man and reform. The collective generosity of the people was embodied in the loving hearts of the men portrayed in *Upbuilders.*

Steffens called this combination of knowing and loving "applied Christianity." It was the "putting into practice in actual life, and in all places . . . the doctrine of faith, hope and charity." Reform was simply the application of the Golden Rule to all social and political activity. "If we loved our neighbor as ourselves we would not then betray, rob and bribe him." For many, Steffens admitted, this method of reform appeared impractical, even "revolutionary." This was the measure of how pervasive "evil" was in the American Christian community. These leaders offered the nation a way back to the true and gentle message of the Golden Rule. Born again by "intelligence," they were shining examples of how "applied

Christianity" could reform the heart of the nation. Mark Fagan exemplified these *Upbuilders:* "The man is a Christian, a literal
Christian; no mere member of a church, but a follower of Christ; no
patron of organized charities, but a giver of kindness, sympathy,
love." The only exception was Rudolph Spreckels.[8]

Although he tried, Steffens could not quite bring himself to include Spreckels, the millionaire businessman, in his pantheon of political saints. Spreckels had all the virtues of "will-power, and per-
sistence, and ability" that marked his business class. He was in the
tradition of those captains of industry who both built and robbed
the nation. Having discovered the "system," Spreckels became a
"honest, fearless, young and open eyed" reformer. He was using his
"talent for organization and executive ability to reform in the united cities of America." While put in the service of reform, these
were nevertheless the attributes of the "aristocrat," not the
democratic leader. As a "master manager," Spreckels must be a
boss,—a "good boss," but, nevertheless, a boss. Because his talents
were of the will and the mind, he was a "cold-blooded" antagonist
of evil. "Personally autocratic, unbending, hard," Spreckels had
none of the warmth and sympathy needed for "applied
Christianity."[9]

In almost direct contradistinction to Spreckels stood Judge Ben
Lindsey. For Steffens, the "kids' judge" was the best example and
the greatest practitioner of the application of Christian doctrine to
life and politics. While Spreckels carefully calculated the methods
he used to gain reform, Lindsey "didn't think them out with his
mind. This isn't the way big, human things are done in this big,
human world of ours; they are done with the heart." Like the other
leaders, Lindsey came to understand the "system" from personal
experience. Sitting on the bench hearing juvenile cases, he suddenly
realized that he was presiding over a "system of vengeance and
fear." Roused to action, this "brave, gentle man" began substitut-
ting "the ancient, neglected" methods of Christian generosity in
the treatment of youthful offenders. If his methods were old,
Lindsey's analysis was as new as the emerging social sciences.[10]

By using moralistic language, Steffens managed to introduce
modern social theory into his chapter on Lindsey without
acknowledging it to his audience. According to Steffens, "the judge
says boys are bad because, while they have lots of opportunity to do
wrong, they have none to do good." From his investigation of the
causes of juvenile crime, Lindsey reached the "conclusion that the

typical environment of an average Christian community was such that even little children could not be good." In short, there were no "bad" children, only bad environments. Improving the surroundings of the child was the cure for juvenile delinquency. For young offenders, the answer was correction, not retribution. This mixing of environmental social theory with religious rhetoric was intentional. The observations of the social scientists, as conveyed through Lindsey, lost their objective neutrality and became the instruments of reform. At the same time, environmentalism explained why the human inclination for good was thwarted by society. If the "conditions which men create" were the source of evil, then man's nature was free of the taint of corruption.[11]

While sociology served its purpose, Steffens was not about to let modern social theory replace Christianity as the keystone of reform. Theories put into practice became institutions, and the organization of an idea inevitably did more harm than good. For Steffens, man was always "inventing devices to help him be a man; a spear, an army, the Church, political parties, business. By and by the aid to his weakness comes to be a fetish with him, a burden, an end in itself, an institution." This was the central paradox of civilization. Organizations were the "natural" creations of men, but once established, institutions became the masters, not the servants, of their creators. Developed to protect and improve society, institutions eventually absorbed "all the loyalty of the members, turning them from and often against the home, the law, and the State." For Steffens, institutions substituted the personal interests of the individual for the universal good of the community. The "institutional idea" made men willing to "sacrifice civilization—for no less is at stake—for their church, their party, or their grocery store."[12]

Steffens was going far beyond his previous criticism of modern American society. Until *Upbuilders,* he had condemned the systematic organization of evil in the nation. Now, he was strongly suggesting that any institution, no matter what its purpose, was a source of corruption. This argument brought Steffens close to anarchism, but his solution was his own brand of pragmatism. For Steffens, "applied Christianity" was the best way of restoring institutions, those edifices of selfishness, to their original purposes. As a Christian, Judge Lindsey was "reintroducing into life, all life, and into all institutions which he can influence, the spirit of humanity." The disposition to treat one's fellow man by the Golden Rule could not be organized into an institution. This proclivity for good prevented the instruments of life from becoming the goals of human existence. The "Christ-spirit of unselfish love" made church, politics, and business "not institutions, but the means to those higher ends, character and right living." By their practice of Christian ethics, Lindsey and the other reform leaders were reducing institutions to their "proper, humble function—the service of men and the State." Steffens was so sure that this was the only path to meaningful reform that he was willing to try it himself. By the time that *Upbuilders* was published, Steffens was already in Boston testing "applied Christianity."[13]

Steffens was in Boston at the request of Edward A. Filene, innovative retailer, millionaire, eccentric, and reformer. Put simply, Filene wanted Steffens to investigate corruption in Boston, rouse its citizens to action, and offer suggestions for reform. For this, Filene would pay Steffens the princely sum of $10,000. Unmindful of the enormity of the task, Steffens accepted the challenge and moved himself and his family to Boston for a year, beginning in October 1908. Steffens plunged into the assignment with unbridled enthusiasm. "It's the biggest piece of work I ever attempted," he told his father, "and I have a dim hope that it may lead me to the establishment by me of a profession, a new calling; that of a city manager or municipal architect." Here was involvement in "real politics," and Steffens loved it. Lecturing, writing, and teaching, he caused a terrific stir and briefly became Boston's foremost celebrity. He tried to bring "intelligence" to both "the most selfish men in the community" and to Harvard students. In this he had some success, but his triumphs ended there.[14]

By the end of his stay in Boston, his effort to guide that city to reform was already headed for certain failure. "Real politics," it seemed, did not lead to real reform. Filene's Good Government Association, an alliance of civic, trade, and business groups, produced "Boston—1915" in the spring of 1909. This was a six year plan for the political and physical revitalization of the city. Despite Steffens' support, "Boston—1915" was a timid document that offered only the mildest of reforms. Although he had little to do with the initial drawing up of the plan, Steffens had to share the blame for its eventual failure. Part of his agreement with Filene called for Steffens to produce a social and political blueprint for the reformers. When finally completed by Steffens in 1914, almost four years late, the manuscript was only an unhappy reminder of what might have been.[15]

While Steffens could not find a publisher for the entire

manuscript, he did manage to have parts of it published as a series in *Metropolitan Magazine* in the first months of 1914. Under the general title, "A Cure For Corruption," Steffens explained his personal effort to apply his theory of knowing and loving to the reform of Boston. Arriving in that city, he found "little vitality of any sort. There is degeneracy; not only political, moral and mental, but physical as well." To revive Boston, Steffens worked from the simple premise that *"good will, inspired, is good."* The people of Boston needed to substitute "a desire for the welfare of all" for the hope of gaining personal "privileges" from society. This could only be done by enlisting the support of all the leaders of Boston, "good men or bad," in the movement for reform. In order to accomplish this end, Steffens tried to "develop in all the people . . . social vision; hope and faith and charity; hope on earth, faith in God and—understanding of the things that make the other fellow do such bad things as we all do." Steffens gave the people and leaders of Boston his "vision" and yet the plan failed; Steffens knew the reason, economics.[16]

As Steffens saw it, a good part of Boston's problem was the unequal distribution of property. In this regard, he took his ideas from the radical American social philosopher Henry George. Steffens had learned the philosophy of the single tax from George's disciples, among them Tom Johnson. Steffens summarized their argument succinctly: "The first earnings of all labor have to go to the landlord, who, neither himself, nor his father, nor his grandfather, made the land. And what is worst, the people whose presence made the site value of that land and whose increase in numbers increased the site value of that land, have to pay interest on the increase they caused, they and they alone. No wonder the people are poor." The consequence was a "useless class of landlords" whose "sin" was to live off the fruits of the labor of others. The solution of the single taxers was a form of expropriation of property, a one hundred percent tax on the unearned increment of income on all land. Steffens did not offer this or any other specific proposal for the redistribution of wealth. But he did insist that *"the object of any reform in Boston must be to keep for Boston all values created by the people of Boston as a community and let the people as individuals get and keep all that they produce—all—and no more."* Nevertheless, Steffens considered the problem of land, while important, to be only the tip of the iceberg.[17]

What the people of Boston could not see, what the nation failed to comprehend, was that business was behind political corruption and social selfishness. In a series written shortly after his Boston experiment, Steffens again took up muckraking to expose this danger to the American people. Yet Steffens' analysis was not so much economic as it was institutional in character. Professing a growing distaste for capitalism, Steffens was really cultivating his profound suspicion of all organized activity. Business was controlled by Wall Street and "It," as Steffens called the financial center of the nation, was "the most vital, the most perfect, and the most powerful part of organized life in human society in America, not excepting the United States government." If Wall Street controlled business, then J. Pierpont Morgan, the investment banker, ruled "It." This made him no less than "the boss of the United States." [18]

Morgan and the other "bosses" of Wall Street controlled the finances of the nation. Through their ability to regulate credit, "the very crown of financial power," they corrupted and controlled American politics. Yet, this was not the ultimate source of their "enormous" influence; "it is sovereign, the money power, but the money power is not based on money; not alone; certainly not on 'their money.' It is founded upon the control of men, presidents of companies, directors, stockholders, depositors, and the public." This "management of men" made business more pernicious than any other kind of organization. All institutions were powerful deflectors of the allegiance of men from the common good to their particular and exclusive interests. Because of the centralized and pervasive character of business, Wall Street not only corrupted men, but commanded them to do its selfish bidding. [19]

Steffens finally recognized himself what was already evident in his writing. He was an anarchist, a Christian anarchist, who, despite his failure in Boston, remained anxious to test his solution for America's social ills. Dynamite gave him his chance. In October 1910, an explosion ripped through the *Los Angeles Times* building, leaving twenty men dead. The bombing signaled open class warfare between capital and labor in Los Angeles. The owner and publisher of the *Times*, General Harrison Gray Otis, was the most outspoken opponent of organized labor in that city. The two men accused of the bombing, John J. McNamara and his brother James, were officers in the International Association of Bridge and Structural Iron Workers. This union had a well-deserved reputation for using dynamite as a method of persuasion. The city, tense and divided, awaited the trial, which promised to be a test of strength between capital and labor, the rich and the poor. Steffens arrived in Los Angeles to cover the proceedings for a newspaper syndicate. He ended up trying to make peace between the two sides.[20]

The guilt or innocence of the two men did not much interest Steffens. In fact, he presumed from the start that the brothers had planted the bomb; his "real purpose was to turn the already pointed general interest in the case into an inquiry into the wrongs done labor, and so to get at the causes of class hate." In preparing for the trial, Clarence Darrow, the defense attorney, reached the same conclusion as Steffens. His clients were guilty and, if brought to trial, would surely hang for their crime. Darrow's despair was Steffens' opportunity. He proposed to save the McNamaras by making a bargain with the antilabor leaders. In return for a plea of guilty by the brothers, the court would treat the two men with great leniency—perhaps even letting them go without punishment. This would be followed by a conference between the leaders of capital and labor where the two sides might use the Golden Rule to replace class warfare with social harmony. With little to lose, Darrow gave Steffens his "chance to make an experiment with 'big, bad men' and with Christianity."[21]

At first, everything went well for Steffens. Sure of "Christianity as a working principle," Steffens preached the "doctrine of forgiveness instead of punishment" to the business and antilabor leaders of Los Angeles. To everyone's surprise except, of course, Steffens, these "sinners" enthusiastically agreed to the plan. Even General Otis, whose building was bombed and employees killed, supported in his own "fierce" way leniency for the McNamaras and mediation of labor strife. There were some bad moments in the negotiations. When Darrow was accused of trying to bribe a juror, the prosecution hardened its demands. With misgivings, the McNamaras and Darrow accepted the stiffer terms of life imprisonment for John and a long jail sentence for his brother. Despite such problems, Steffens managed to keep the settlement patched together with the aid of the "practical men of business and politics." For Steffens, this was a vindication of his belief that there was "enough good will in all men of imagination and power to do any good, hard job."[22]

The McNamaras' plea of guilty caused a sensation, and Steffens anxiously awaited the response of Los Angeles and the nation. If the people did not appreciate what had been done, all was lost. The key to public opinion was the churches; thus, the Sunday following the confession of guilt was the "decisive day." According to the bitterly disappointed Steffens, the religious community did not understand "the fact that Christianity had been applied and worked." Instead of forgiveness, the churches preached "hatred and disappointed revenge." Despite the storm of protest that followed the righteous, unforgiving sermons, the "leading capitalist and employers . . . stood fast" in support of the Golden Rule. It was the "heelers, the mere followers who will not think or act without a leader to direct them," who broke and ran and took the judge in the case with them. On the day of sentencing, the judge expressed the sentiment of the "churches and public opinion." He denounced the McNamaras and went back on the agreement made between capital and labor. Leaving the courtroom, one of the brothers turned to Steffens and said, " 'You see? You were wrong, and I was right. The whole damn world believes in dynamite.' " For the second time in three years, Steffens had failed to make "applied Christianity" work in practical affairs.[23]

Despite their failure, these experiments were important and necessary for Steffens. He was sure that the intellectual was incapable of doing anything truly effective for society. To write, the journalist must be a thinker who doubted and questioned the world around him. Good journalism was essentially "open-minded thinking in public." Obviously, Steffens did this well, but he was often uncomfortable with this role. This was not the virtue of the man of action. As Steffens saw it, the bold leader, once he made up his mind, had to be "blind" to any alternatives to his chosen course. As a mover and shaker of events, he could not "doubt, think, and consciously learn in action." He did not use his brain to reflect, but as a "muscle to drive something home." In his effort, "to bring about an essential change in the American mind," Steffens tried valiantly to combine both roles. The process of moving the American mind away from its old, distorted perspective called for reflection and skepticism, the talents of the intellectual. The creation of a new "vision" for the nation demanded commitment and action, the virtues of the leader. For Steffens, the two roles were not of equal importance in society. If he had learned anything in Boston, it was that only leaders "give life to—anything." The McNamara case taught him the bitter truth that he might be a prophet, but never a ruler of events.[24]

Feeling "defeated, disgraced somehow, helpless," Steffens returned to New York. Labor leaders considered his interference with the trial, at best, "folly" and, at worst, "treason." To capitalists, Steffens was little more than an apologist for their enemies. His "experiment" in Los Angeles even cost him his already fading popularity with the public. As a muckraker, he had appeared to be a knight leading an army of millions toward the gates of reform. Now, he resembled a quixotic figure jousting with windmills. He found it very difficult to write, and the articles he managed to complete were "regularly returned, often unread" from his former publishers. Steffens suffered greatly from his loss of eminence as a journalist, and his efforts to regain his old position, if touching, bordered on the pathetic. In early 1914, he won a five hundred dollar prize for answering George Bernard Shaw's article, "A Case for Equality," in *Metropolitan Magazine*. In the hope of starting a debate with the brilliant English author that might be carried by *Metropolitan*, Steffens tried "to egg him on." The trouble was that nobody was listening to either Steffens or the call for reform.[25]

In some ways, progressivism began to decline soon after the election of 1908. Roosevelt's own choice as his successor, William Howard Taft, proved to be a timid president who eventually sided with the conservative forces in Congress. A year later, the elections swept from office many of the leading urban reformers. Even Tom Johnson lost in Cleveland, and Steffens tried to console his old friend. Comparing Johnson to Moses, Steffens gently reminded Johnson that all great men "suffered when it came home finally to them that they might see but never could go over into the Land of Promise." Bitter and spent, Johnson died within two years. The final fling of reform came in 1912 with Roosevelt's return to the center of the political stage. First he stole, much to Steffens' disgust, the banner of progressivism from LaFollette. Unable to wrestle the Republican nomination for president from Taft, Roosevelt and his Republican supporters organized their own party. Steffens did not join this magnificient, futile crusade. He stood detached, bemused, and skeptical on the sidelines of the conflict. For Steffens, reform politics were old, tired, and useless. Steffens had already embarked on a new life.[26]

New York and youth gave Lincoln Steffens his new beginning. In January 1911, Josephine died after a long illness. "Lost" in grief and "helpless" without a wife who had managed his affairs for twenty years, Steffens moved to Greenwich Village. This old, dilapidated, working class section of New York was the new mecca for "young poets, and painters, playwrights, actors, and Bohemians, and labor leaders of a radical trend." Taking a room on Washington Square, Steffens watched, and soon joined, this volatile, temporary mixture of social and political radicalism. In the apartment above his lived the young poet and writer John Reed, whom Steffens had met at Harvard. Steffens became Reed's gentle and understanding mentor—a surrogate father. In turn, Reed, "a big, growing, happy being," helped the now middle-aged journalist regain his exuberance for life. For Reed, "every new experience, sight, and idea" was the "most wonderful thing in the world." It became the same for Steffens. The Village was the place for the young and the young of spirit "to live and be free."[27]

Presiding over the whole diverse and colorful scene was Mabel Dodge. Wealthy socialite, freethinker, disciple of Freud and Jung, political and cultural radical, she epitomized the eclectic and free spirit of the Village before World War I. With the "courage of inexperience," she did anything that it "struck her fancy to do, and put it and herself over—openly." Her apartment, at Steffens' suggestion, became a salon where anyone and everyone met to discuss everything and anything. The "reds"—Emma Goldman, Max Eastman, and Floyd Dell—lectured and argued the differences between anarchism and socialism. Big Bill Haywood, the notorious leader of the Industrial Workers of the World, held forth on the virtues of industrial violence and the merits of direct action in labor disputes. Walter Lippmann, another Steffens protégé from Harvard, related psychoanalysis to the practice of morality and politics. The conversations were charged with a sense of discovery and the anticipation of the coming liberation of man and society.[28]

The prophets of this dawning age of freedom were Marx and Freud. Steffens already knew enough about Marxism to agree that the class system was the root of social injustice. Freud was a different matter. For American radicals, the Viennese philosopher was teaching both men and women how to tear away the suffocating layers of bourgeois culture that strangled physical and creative human expression. Steffens was more interested in the social and political implications of psychoanalysis than in the unleashing of his own passions. Listening and learning, Steffens thought "how absurd had been my muckraker's descriptions of bad men and good men and the assumption that showing people the facts and conditions could persuade them to alter them or their own conduct." Freudian theory agreed with the Marxist insistence that

"to change men's minds one must first change their environment."
Made a radical by Christianity, Marx and Freud helped make
Steffens a gentle revolutionary.[29]

CHAPTER 6

South of the Border

A T the beginning of World War I, Steffens was in Europe.
Ostensibly, he was there to muckrake European politics and
government. For him, the industrial nations of the Old World were
the harbingers of the American future. In varying degrees, they
were all in the advanced stages of the corrupt system Steffens had
so vividly described in American cities and states. The leaders and
bosses of Europe no longer ever pretended to separate politics and
government from business and profits. The British saw government
by and for privilege as proper; they had even given it a veneer of
respectability. On the other hand, the French made no pretensions
of moral superiority. Instead, they accepted the cold, hard truth of
an unfair world. Cynically, they recognized the corruption of
government by economic interests as the inevitable price of security. As intelligent realists, the French only sought to forestall the
collapse of this rotten system as long as possible. Revealing this
bleak future needed to be done, but not by Steffens: "How could
one make a young, vigorous, optimistic people on a virgin, rich part
of the earth's surface look ahead to those old peoples on old ground
and see the road we were on would lead up over the hill and down
to Rome, Egypt, or China?"[1]

Accepting this vision was as difficult for Steffens as it was for his
fellow countrymen. By 1914, Steffens had lost some of his American
innocence, but he still retained a firm, obstinate faith in the ultimate improvement of mankind. For Americans, the essence of life
was progress, and Steffens believed this as much as any of his contemporaries. The advancement of individual and national fortune
was the path to personal and social well-being. As a result, Steffens'
articles and essays continued to be both a description and a part of
the social transformation he found in his investigations. He identified his own vitality with the swift currents of change around him.
For Steffens, visiting decadent Europe was little more than a

"moral rest." Although it was comfortable, Steffens could not remain too long in Europe. To live and work in a dying culture meant that Steffens himself was no longer truly alive. His commitment to revolution was as much a personal necessity as it was a product of social observation.[2]

Steffens believed that the popular evolutionary social theories of this period supported his contention that society was ever advancing—transforming itself into some better form. Organized human activity was an organism that had little choice but to obey the evolutionary laws that had little choice but to obey the evolutionary laws that carried it forward in an inevitable progression. By using the "laws of biology and sociology," Steffens sought to recapture the scientific approach that he first embraced in his student days. For too long, Steffens told Allen H. Suggett, his brother-in-law, he had been too "personal and emotional" in his investigation of "human conduct." It had been a "rich study," Steffens admitted, but it had cost him his objectivity. Now, by studying society in a scientific manner, Steffens hoped to understand the evolutionary laws that governed society and, thereby, to glimpse the future of man. This could not be done in Europe. For Steffens, the Old World was at the end of an exhausted phase of human development. As the lights of that civilization went out, Steffens dallied for awhile and then went home.[3]

His incredulous colleagues were "astonished" by this decision. General war in Europe was the single most important event to take place in Western civilization in the last one hundred years. In fact, Steffens had made an intelligent and correct decision. He understood both himself and the significance of the conflict better than his friends. Steffens realized that the war would yield little for him as a writer. War correspondent was the profession of young men who had the stamina and youthful imagination to see and feel the battle. Behind the lines, Steffens would be just another journalist intentionally or, in his case, unintentionally stirring the passions of the American people for war. In any case, the war was an "incomprehensible, barbarous mix-up." There would be little to witness until it was over. When peace returned to Europe, Steffens would be there to understand the "significance" of this act of mass social suicide. Until then, he would prepare himself for what he was sure would be the inevitable consequence of the fighting—revolution. To this end, Steffens set out "to make a study of revolutions."[4]

Mexico was the place to begin this work. An underdeveloped nation, Mexico was in the midst of civil war and revolution. Most Americans dismissed this struggle as simply another example of what they considered their Latin neighbors' childish, almost comical, tantrums. American radicals were not much more sympathetic with the Mexicans and their revolution. Some, adhering to Marxist ideology, refused to recognize any revolution that took place in a nation that had not yet reached the industrial stage of development. Young American radicals, including John Reed, saw the civil war as a romantic saga, with Pancho Villa, the picturesque general turned bandit, as the hero of the drama. Steffens would accept none of these preconceived generalizations. He abhorred the American public's sense of moral, racial, and social superiority. Unable to confine himself to any doctrinaire position, Steffens saw no reason why the Mexicans could not have a real revolution. Older and more experienced than Reed, he did not share his friend's entrancement with the sight of marching troops set against the brilliance of a Mexican sunset. Without prejudice and ideology, Steffens went to Mexico in November 1914 to observe the Mexicans and learn about revolutions. The result was a series of insightful articles about the Mexican revolution. Since then, these pieces have become almost timeless guides to the nature of revolutions in this century and the tragic American response to them.[5]

In his idyllic portrayal, Mexico came close to being a "Garden of Eden." The earth was so rich and the seas so bountiful that Mexico "might be a heaven." According to Steffens, the people did not have to work very hard to live comfortably: "One day's light labor a week or an hour or two a day brings forth all the fruit, fish, and flowers—all the food, shelter, and clothing they have to have." Consequently, Steffens explained, the Mexicans cared little for wealth and profits but much for the good life their generous land afforded them. Quickly done with the drudgery of work, they could "loaf and play, make love and war or a useful tool beautiful . . . and they are able to do such things happily." So romanticized was Steffens' description that the Mexicans appeared to be little more than "children" of nature. At first glance, this suggests that, unconsciously, Steffens was being at least a bit condescending toward the Mexicans. In fact, Steffens purposely overemphasized the simplicity of the Mexicans in order to make quite a different point.[6]

Steffens believed that Americans could learn much from the Mexicans. His glowing descriptions of Mexican culture were not very subtle criticisms of life in the United States. In "Smith of

Guanajuato," which appeared as "Those Lazy Mexicans" in *Hearst's International* in May 1922, Steffens compared the United States to Rome and Mexico to Greece. Like the Romans, the Americans devoted all their energies to gaining "riches." With the ancient Greeks, the Mexicans were an "aesthetic" people who loved beauty. For Mexicans, work must be an act of creation; for Americans, it was a means to wealth and profit. The Americans, according to Steffens, were a "moral" people who could not enjoy their labor. On the other hand, the Mexicans could not "distinguish between work and play." The virtues of cooperation between the two nations were obvious to Steffens. The Americans could show the Mexicans how to create wealth; the Mexicans could teach the Americans how to enjoy doing it. Most Americans never even considered this possibility. Like the other foreigners in Mexico, the Americans, Steffens sadly reported, did not even try to understand Mexico and its people. For Steffens, the Americans as well as the French, Germans, and English were far more than rude, insensitive visitors, they were the "serpent in this Garden."[7]

In a terse, bold style reminiscent of his muckraking days, Steffens described the exploitation of poor, innocent Mexico by the industrial nations of the world. The foreigners cared nothing for the beauty of this sun-drenched land. Instead, they saw "the fruit of the tree and the ore in the ground" and thought only of ways to exploit them. Through bribery, promises, and intimidation, these foreign investors gained the right to develop Mexico's vast resources. Yet, robbing Mexico of its natural wealth did not satisfy these alien businessmen. Besides this crime, the incensed journalist accused them of causing untold human suffering among the Mexican people. As Steffens explained it, the foreigners needed laborers, but found the Mexicans to be less than willing workers. Happy on their small land holdings, the Mexicans saw no reason to sweat and die in foreign-owned mines. With the aid of the Mexican government, the Mexican farmer was driven off his land and forced, by the threat of starvation, to work for these alien employers. According to Steffens, even this was not enough. Needing little money, the peons worked only sporadically. To discipline their work force, the Americans, Germans, English, and French forced the peons into debt. The result was a "form of slavery" that was, by Steffens' estimation, roughly equivalent to the sharecropping system of the American South. Finally, the foreign investor had an oppressed but dependable labor force. They had their profits, and Mexico had its poor and discontented millions.[8]

Steffens recognized that none of this could have happened without the help of at least some portion of Mexico's ruling class. He understood how what now would be called a neocolonial elite was formed in Mexico. Porfirio Diaz, dictator of Mexico before the revolution, was the architect of this alliance between Mexico's native elite and the foreign investors. Ironically, Diaz himself was the product of an earlier revolution that freed his people from the adventurer Santa Anna. For Steffens, Diaz was a tragic figure. A "great," even a "good" man, he had been led astray by his efforts to attain two illusionary goals. After his accession to power, Diaz desperately wanted to restore order to Mexico. According to Steffens, Diaz was willing to pay too high a price for peace. In return for an opportunity to loot the countryside, the "boldest bandits" in Mexico became his brutal police force. To win the loyalty of the upper classes, Diaz granted them "concessions and privileges, more and more of his power, the riches and labor and the loyalty of his people." All this was very familiar to Steffens. Like so many other leaders, Diaz had taken the "easy" path to power. In the process, he had "unknowingly" sold out both himself and his people to the privileged classes. In turn, they sold Mexico to foreign investors.[9]

The apple this foreign "serpent" offered Diaz and his "friends" was money. Despite its natural riches, Mexico was a poor country and Diaz and his supporters needed funds to sustain their corrupt "system." Foreign interests were more than happy to invest their capital in this oppressed but peaceful land with its wealth of untapped resources. Still, before they would modernize Mexico, these investors demanded that Diaz accept "foreign ideas and ideals, foreign methods, policies, rights" as well as foreign money. As Steffens described it, the vicious "system" was not complete.

He . . . would let them get hold of the gold, silver, oil and other incredibly rich natural resources of Mexico, they would divide profits with him and his ring; lend his treasury all the money he wanted (at a high rate of interest and with bankers, brokers, and all sorts of commissions to divide up); and they would (and they did) corrupt and keep corrupt all the powerful men in his government and generally develop the country; not the people, but the land, mines, etc.

The use of the "scientific" methods of the industrial nations satisfied everyone involved in the "system." Diaz was secure in power, and his "friends" had their graft. The foreign capitalists reaped enormous profits from their investments. Steffens saw the fatal flaw in this apparently successful exploitation of Mexico and its people. As the Mexican upper classes grew ever wealthier, they became more dependent on foreign money, influence, and power. The "serpent" had taken over the "garden." This was too much for the "silent, smiling, polite, patient, grave" people of Mexico. They rose up in revolution.[10]

Steffens reminded his American audience that this "system" was not very different from the one he had described in the United States during his muckraking days. In fact, Steffens found striking parallels between the two:

There was Diaz, president and boss (McKinley and Hanna) in one, with his corrupt but able political ring, and the powerful business and clerical ring back of it, which cast and counted the votes of the people, and used their power and their pitiful faith to get and sell or give away concessions, lands, mines, oil claims—privileges. . . . Thus the Mexican Republic came to represent not the people, but the banks and concessionaires, both Mexican and foreign, the public-service corporations, the breweries and saloons, gambling houses and lotteries, prostitution (organized), contractors, landlords, and all persons, classes, and businesses privileged to break or be above the law.

According to Steffens, the only real difference between the two systems was that Diaz was forced to "import his financiers." In one sense, Steffens used this comparison to condemn the "business system" wherever it was in power. This was a mild and not very effective attack on capitalism. His larger purpose was to explain Mexico and the causes of the revolution in terms that could be easily understood by his readers. This was typical of Steffens. Whether describing St. Louis or Mexico, Steffens was willing to sacrifice complexity for clarity. He did not want to impress his audience with the sophistication of his analysis; his goal was always to convey some important social truth to his readers. By comparing Mexico to the United States, he simplified his argument in the hope that Americans might better appreciate Mexico. For all his faith in the power of knowledge, Steffens was fully aware that American familiarity with the Mexican situation would not necessarily make the United States any more sympathetic to the plight of Mexico.[11]

Steffens rightly understood that the United States had a blind spot for the rest of the world. Born in the wilderness and raised to nationhood by revolution, the American people could not imagine a more advanced or progressive nation than their own. As the light of the world, the United States found it inconceivable that any other society could offer it anything of consequence. Smug in their superiority, Americans saw no reason why they should try to understand the shrinking, changing world of the twentieth century. Steffens used the example of Mexico to teach the American people of their own ignorance and dangerous arrogance. Americans must recognize, Steffens warned, that "the Mexicans are a different people, of a different breed, in a different stage of development, in a different environment, with different traditions and very different ideals." If the United States did not learn "the mystery of Mexico," Steffens predicted tragic consequences. At best, the United States would have to live with the hatred of her southern neighbor; at worst, American's persistent arrogance meant war.[12]

Steffens was very careful how he presented these criticisms to the American people. He chose not to confront his readers directly with his accusations. Instead, he brilliantly adopted the use of the dramatic dialogue, a literary tool he often used in his work, to serve his purpose. In "The Sunny Side of Mexico" published in *Metropolitan Magazine* in May 1915, Steffens described an interview he supposedly had with a Wall Street financier. As always, Steffens posed as the knowledgeable but willing seeker of the truth. While Steffens certainly slanted the discussion to his advantage, his subject was given the opportunity to defend the position of American investors in Mexico. Superficially, then, the discussion appeared to be a fair exchange of views between two reasonable men. In fact, the businessman was little more than a straw man set up by Steffens. Nevertheless, by making his argument within the context of this interview, Steffens ameliorated some of the harshness of his criticisms of American attitudes toward Mexico without sacrificing any of their substance.

According to Steffens, this Wall Street businessman "knew Mexico from the inside." The financier begins the interview "grimly" by insisting that the United States must intervene in the Mexican revolution. This was necessary because that nation had collapsed into a state of chaos, with the armies of the opposing factions marching through the countryside looting, destroying property, and murdering innocent people. Steffens interrupts to inquire if the man was speaking of Europe. This was a sharp rejoinder. At this stage of World War I, few Americans had any desire to interfere in a war that was literally killing millions of men in the trenches of

France and on the open plains of Poland. If Americans really wanted to stop " 'barbarism [and] savagery'," the logical place to start was rich, civilized Europe and not poor, supposedly primitive, "weak" Mexico. With the exchange, Steffens made the hypocrisy of interfering in the affairs of less fortunate regions of the world devastatingly clear. Taken aback by this remark, the businessman hesitated for a moment and then responded with a "laugh." Satisfied that Steffens was not really serious, the financier went on to tell a "typical gringo's tale."[13]

"Americans abroad," Steffens observed, "seem to become un-American." Wall Street supported and applauded the brutal suppression of the Mexican people by Diaz and his government. His methods were direct; " 'no judges, no juries, no—poppycock. Just a word and a volley.' " This, of course, was Steffens' exaggeration of the position of American businessmen, but it did tell an essential truth. Americans were all too ready to support repressive measures in other countries in order to accomplish American aims. The financier agreed with Steffens' assessment that Mexico was a "Garden of Eden," and that, according to his way of thinking, was the trouble with it. Left to themselves, the Mexicans would never develop their resources. American businessmen were sure that an American future was best for Mexico. The financier assured Steffens that with American capital and Diaz's methods, Mexico " 'could be made a United States, only richer, much greater.' " Here Steffens was touching on one of the central assumptions that guided American business and governmental relations with other nations. Without question, most Americans simply assumed that the rest of the globe wanted, or should want, to be like the United States.[14]

For Steffens, this was an unwarranted assumption. For one thing, it was the height of national arrogance to insist that all peoples of the globe would, if given the opportunity, adopt American economic, social, and political institutions. He asked, " 'wouldn't it be better, to let the Mexicans see if they can't develop along other lines toward some other ideal, to perhaps a better civilization?' " Besides, the United States, as Steffens' own investigations of local, state, and federal corruption had shown, had enough problems to keep her busy without becoming involved in the internal affairs of Mexico or, for that matter, those of any other country. These arguments were not new; they were part of the standard criticism of American foreign policy in the early twentieth century. While Steffens accepted their validity, he was not satisfied to stop with them. In his articles and essays about Mexico, he added his own u-nique contribution to the traditional criticism of American involvement abroad.[15]

Steffens recognized the contradiction in the effort to make Mexico or any other country like the United States. By supporting dictators such as Diaz, Americans were making it impossible for any nation to adopt American political or social institutions. Defending himself and his colleagues, the Wall Street financier insisted that American business interests were only following the customs of Mexico. Steffens dismissed this as fallacious reasoning. As Steffens saw it, a good part of the "awful customs" of the Mexican government were a direct result of foreign involvement. Impatiently, Steffens reduced the whole American argument to its basic absurdity: the Mexicans were corrupt, so investors made then more corrupt in order to make them more like Americans. Put this way, Steffens saw only two choices for American investors. If they were corrupting Mexico to make it more like the United States, then they must admit that American society was worse than Mexico's. On the other hand, they could confess that their argument was a sham and that it was only a rationale for their exploitation of Mexico. Either way, the Mexicans gained nothing from American interference.[16]

This analysis led Steffens to make a startling observation. He tentatively suggested that American support for such "un-American" activities abroad was an expression of a covert desire to act in the same manner at home. Perhaps, Diaz only did in Mexico what many American businessmen wanted some strong leader to do in the United States. By methods that could never be sanctioned by American laws or ideals, the Mexican dictator kept order and protected business against its labor and radical opponents. The niceties and demands of a constitutional democracy were often wearisome burdens for many. Consequently, some American businessmen looked fondly upon a simpler, more direct, less democratic method of dealing with internal conflict. Steffens did not, could not, develop the implications of this disturbing insight. It was the seed of an idea that, from the perspective of time and events, would reach its full fruition in the 1960s. In *The Armies Of The Night*, Norman Mailer, apparently unaware of Steffens' initial contribution, used the concept to explain American involvement in Vietnam. Unable to cope with their own children and the complexity of a technological society, Americans looked abroad to purge their nightmare. According to Mailer, the frustrations of American

life "traveled on the nozzle tip of a flame thrower" to kill in a surrogate manner in the steaming jungles those who could not be
morally or legally destroyed at home.[17]

In 1915, Steffens was ready to concede that American intervention was more than an expression of suppressed atavism or a selfish
desire for wealth. The United States often intervened in Latin
America with the best and most generous of motives. As he noted,
monuments to American engineering and scientific sanitation were
to be found everywhere in the Caribbean. Yet the Latin Americans
hated the United States. With great tact, Steffens explained why.
Again in "The Sunny Side of Mexico," Steffens used an interview to
make his point. This time, his subject was an intelligent, upper class
Havana newspaper editor. The suspicious Cuban was initially unwilling to talk about American foreign policy with Steffens. This
was a clever literary ploy on the part of Steffens. He knew that most
Americans would find a harsh attack on their foreign policy by a
foreigner, especially a Cuban, offensive. At the same time, Steffens
believed that it was both fitting and necessary that just such an individual reveal why even friendly intervention made more enemies
than friends for the United States. Consequently, the reluctant
editor only made his feelings known after much prodding by
Steffens. For the Cuban people, the editor explained to Steffens,
the United States was like a stranger who came into another man's
house and " 'found it not to his taste.' " Instead of leaving the
home alone, " 'the stranger cleaned it all up, cleaned and ran the
whole family for a while.' " It was the very act of intervention, not
just the kind of intervention, that the Cubans so much resented.[18]

Steffens, of course, found this explanation most reasonable. No
matter how noble the motives, "intervention is interference, and
the resentment of interference is human." Steffens reminded
Americans that they certainly felt the same way. Americans would
not stand for, say, German interference in their way of life. The
same held true for the Cubans or the Mexicans. In Steffens' opinion, this hostility to foreign interference was the ultimate cause of
the Mexican revolution. Still, Steffens warned, too many Americans
had not learned this lesson. American investors in Mexico wanted to
stop the revolution and restore the old "system" that had been so
profitable for them. At the other extreme, President Woodrow
Wilson was ready to intervene for what he and other liberals
thought was the good of the Mexicans. An exasperated Steffens explained to the president that it was impossible to "commit rape a

little." For Steffens, the idealistic Wilson was as much a victim of American blindness as any greedy investor.[19]

In his *Autobiography,* Steffens examined why it was so difficult for President Wilson to "hold to his course" in regard to Mexico. Steffens had no doubts about the president's good intentions. As a liberal, Wilson believed in national self-determination, and yet he found it almost impossible to resist the pressure to intervene in Mexico. According to Steffens, the reason was simple, and his analysis remains as apropos today as it was then. Even at this early stage, Steffens realized that the modern presidency isolated its holder. Like any executive, the president could only make decisions based on the information given him by his subordinates. In the case of Mexico, the officers of the State Department had the "duty and machinery to furnish facts" to Wilson. Steffens accused them of supplying the president, not with the truth, but with "criminal mis-information." Blinded by their own prejudices, these agents of the president only reported the facts that supported their preconceived notions. Misled and "alone," Wilson almost stumbled into war with Mexico. Fortunately, Steffens, as an unofficial emissary of the Mexican government, was able to correct Wilson's false impressions about the Mexican revolution. He still had enough faith in the "democratic sympathy of the American people" to believe that, given the truth, they would side with the Mexican cause.[20]

"A revolution," Steffens argued, "is a confusing, fierce, and revolting force." As Steffens described it, the Mexican revolution was no different. It was a joyful, bloody, painful process of giving birth to a new society. Steffens made no effort to minimize the cost to those who were driven from power. The possessions of the old order became the playthings of the revolution. In Vera Cruz, Steffens watched "officers, high and low, soldiers, civil officials, peons and the families of peons; even Yaqui Indians—all classes, except only the leisure class, . . . riding, fast, and noisily, and gaily, up and down the narrow, little, old streets." Every vehicle had been stolen from the Mexican rich, and all the foreign observers objected to this thievery and "anarchy." Steffens agreed that it was anarchy, but he approved of this strange, colorful parade. " '[A] stolen auto going full speed through a jolly crowd' " symbolized the newly found freedom of the Mexican people. For Steffens, this unrestrained euphoria marked only one phase of the revolution. The people must have their joy to prepare themselves for the great sorrows of the struggle.[21]

Unflinchingly, Steffens described the horrors of the revolution. According to Steffens, the revolution could not be satisfied with stealing the automobiles of its enemies. The logic of revolution demanded that the old order be destroyed completely. Yet, the revolution did not control the terrifying force that carried out this necessary end.

When you arm the people they form into armies, and the soldier becomes supreme. The soldier's instincts and his orders are to destroy. But he doesn't destroy what the revolutionist would destroy. The soldier only destroys everything he can lay his hands on. He destroys men, not ideas; women and virtue, not prostitution and vice; buildings, not institutions; courthouses, not injustice; bridges, tracks, and cars, not railroad charters and corruption; growing crops and landlords, not the landlord and unfair land tenure.

In this respect, Steffens understood the dynamics of revolution better than Marx. Armies, he insisted, not revolutionaries, "wrecked the machinery of social living." The revolutionaries could only watch helplessly as the soldiers carried out the atavistic logic of their profession. "Militarism," then, was the inevitable, frightful child of the revolution. For Steffens, it was the "difference" between reform and revolution.[22]

At the same time, Steffens realized that "militarism" posed a deadly threat to the revolution. Everyone suffered from the excesses of the looting, marauding soldiers. "Outraged and in terror of the generals and their armies," the Mexican people demanded an end to war and a return to peace. This, Steffens well understood, was no easy task. Having completed their awful duties, the soldiers were seldom willing graciously to return control of the nation to the revolutionaries. Once generals, men like Pancho Villa became bandits who raped, murdered, and stole in the name of the revolution. If the revolutionaries and their loyal troops did not regain control of the countryside, the revolution was doomed. Tired of violence, the once joyful people would turn against the revolution and look to a dictator to restore order. This, Steffens believed, was the revolutionary process at its most vulnerable moment, and the "emigres" and their foreign allies were ready to take advantage of the situation. Using the growing discontent within Mexico and the foreign revulsion against the excesses of the revolution, these enemies of the revolution tried to force foreign intervention to restore the old system.[23]

This threat presented the revolutionaries with a difficult choice, and according to Steffens, they made the right, in fact the only possible, decision. On the one hand, the revolutionaries could compromise with their foes and have peace for Mexico. This appeared to be a reasonable course of action, but the revolutionaries readily recognized it as a trap. As "historians," they understood the bitter lessons of the past; what was reasonable for the upper classes and their foreign allies was death to the revolution. Diaz, himself a revolutionary, had paid the price for peace and had ended by selling out his people to the privileged few. Francisco Madero, the sensitive, trusting prophet of the present revolution, had willingly listened to his "friends" in high places. "The great landlords, the great concessionaires, the great financiers, the great clergy, the great foreigners" had used him and, when he had served their purposes, killed him. Consequently, the revolutionaries rejected what they knew to be a sham offer of compromise. With Steffens' sympathy, they decided to continue the revolutionary struggle. History gave them no choice.[24]

The discovery of history was as important for Steffens as it was for the Mexican revolutionaries. For all his interest in society and social change, Steffens had never used the discipline of history in his investigations. He had little or no need for it. He judged men and events by standards based on his moral imperatives. The decline of muckraking and progressivism and his experiences in Boston and Los Angeles destroyed his confidence in the social power of morality. Still, Steffens fervently wanted to believe in progress, but he was left without a criteria for measuring it. Revolution was the answer, and history was the engine of social upheaval. Steffens saw human advancement "everywhere" based on the immutable laws of social development. This evolutionary process could only be found by the study of the past. History provided Steffens with a new foundation for his faith in progress. For Steffens, the Mexican revolution and its leaders became the embodiment of these progressive, historical forces as they worked themselves out in human experience.

Steffens' use of history changed his whole perception of strong men. Where once he had portrayed powerful leaders as the shapers of their environments, he now described Venustiano Carranza, the leader of the Mexican revolution, as the servant of events. As described by Steffens, Carranza was not a very formidable or impressive figure. Once merely an "indignant gentleman," he was "converted by . . . events into a relentless revolutionist." Carranza drew his strength and power from the "red flag of revolution," which he picked from the ground upon his friend Madero's death. "Slow, obstinate, unreasonable," he struggled toward the goals of the revolution. In Steffens' opinion, Carranza had little choice. He must follow the logic of history or be destroyed by it. Carranza could not betray the revolution for a moment and hope to "live." In his *Autobiography*, Steffens briefly described, without remorse, the fate of Carranza. When he tried to stop the revolution before it had "run its course . . . a revolutionary party . . . rose against Carranza, caught and shot him, and went on." For Steffens, leaders only survived as long as they rode the "uncontrollable" current of revolution.[25]

In this sense, Steffens became a historical determinist. He believed that the logic of historical events gave the Mexican people little choice but to opt for a radical transformation of their whole social and economic system. For Steffens, the overthrow of the Diaz regime proved the bankruptcy of its policies. Political reform had failed to remedy the intolerable conditions of Mexican life. Every effort to use reform methods to stop corruption and privilege had ended in failure; always, the "old system" returned to power. According to Steffens, history had eliminated every alternative but revolution. Speaking through Carranza, Steffens insisted that Mexico could only be set free by "an economic, not a political revolution." Nevertheless, Steffens saw the real possibility that the revolution could fail. While he believed that the Mexican revolution was a historical necessity, he was not sure of its success.[26]

Unlike Marxist determinists, Steffens did not accept the inevitability of the historical process. Where a true Marxist theoretician studied history in order to resolve social contradictions, Steffens was satisfied to accept the paradoxical lessons of the past. If history taught Steffens the necessity of revolution, it also suggested quite a different and opposite truth to him. Every time the Mexican people tried to eradicate the oppressive system that ruled them, a "strong man, the dictator" rose to restore the old order. In this respect, Steffens found history to be "against" revolution. Steffens could never become a true determinist. He lived in hope, not conviction. Like morality, history gave Steffens a reason to believe in progress, but could not assure the advancement of mankind.[27]

Steffens was optimistic that the Mexican revolution, without outside interference, would succeed for quite another reason. Steffens placed his faith in the Mexican people: "I think it is a key to the understanding of the thorughness, the duration, and the hopefulness of the Mexican revolution that the Mexican people know only what they want." They wanted to end privilege and throw the foreigners out of Mexico, but most of all, they wanted land. Although illiterate and uneducated, the mass of Mexicans intuitively understood that the redistribution of land was the solution to their problems. Steffens argued that their ignorance was a great blessing. Because of it, the Mexican people could not be diverted from their goal by illusory and false promises. Whether he realized it or not, Steffens described the peons as having the same dream as the Jeffersonian yeoman farmer. The ownership of land meant both economic and political independence. They would have no "bosses" to control their lives. In other ways, Steffens explained that the Mexicans wanted a "civilization" much different than the one in the United States. With their leader, Carranza, they shared a vision of a society with "less labor and more play; less thrift and more joyousness; less misery and more—much more general leisure and culture and—happiness."[28]

The achievement of these "high purposes," Steffens knew, was in the future. Steffens could not afford to wait and observe the final triumph of the Mexican revolution. Despite all his sympathy for the Mexicans, his ultimate goal was not the study of any particular revolution. His purpose was to understand the process of revolution as a human, social act. Only by comparative analysis could he turn his impressions into a theory of revolution. This, of course, was the technique that had worked so well for Steffens in his investigations of American municipal, state, and business corruption. Unlike cities though, revolutions were not a continual and permanent part of the social landscape. Still, he was convinced that revolutions would sweep Europe after the war. He wanted to be prepared to understand such a momentous event. Unexpectedly, it was Russia that gave Steffens his opportunity to complete his study of revolutions.

CHAPTER 7

History Turns Red

I N 1917, Steffens witnessed two events that irrevocably changed both his life and the course of modern history. During the first months of that year, the Russian autocracy tottered and then fell under the weight of carrying on a costly, deadly modern war with a primitive economy and an equally backward governmental bureaucracy. One month later, President Woodrow Wilson led the United States into World War I for the announced purpose of ending the necessity of war by making "the world safe for democracy." For the next two years, Lincoln Steffens tried to join these two "young" people together in the pursuit of a better world. First with hope and then with desperation, Steffens attempted to make himself and his writing a positive link between the United States and Russia, liberalism and revolution, and between Wilson and Lenin. As long as his expectations for cooperation or reconciliation remained high, Steffens found no contradictions between the methods and goals of the Russian Revolution and the principles of American liberalism. It was the failure of Wilson at the Paris Peace Conference and Steffens' second visit to Russia that left Steffens a "broken liberal" and an avid apologist for the Bolshevik-led revolution.[1]

American liberals greeted the first news of the Russian Revolution with enthusiasm, and Steffens was, of course, no exception. What distinguished Steffens from other liberals was his opportunity to observe the revolution first hand. In March 1917, Charles Crane, Chicago millionaire and Russian expert, was asked by the Wilson administration to examine the new liberal-revolutionary regime in Russia. By a stroke of good fortune, Steffens ran across his old friend Crane in Washington, and the millionaire asked Steffens to join his small delegation. Without hesitation, Steffens seized this once in a lifetime opportunity to see a revolution in its formative stage. Steffens spent the next six weeks in Russia observing the people,

100

their leaders, and the revolution. Not surprisingly, Steffens returned to the United States with a glowing description of the character and promise of the Russian Revolution.[2]

As always, Steffens found it impossible to separate his social-political vision from his personal needs. He went to Russia with Crane despite the fact that his sister, Lou, lay on her deathbed in California. Steffens asked his other sister, Laura, to understand this apparently unfeeling, selfish decision. Although he was "full of self-accusing and self-defense," Steffens explained to Laura that he simply had to "understand revolutions," and therefore he must go to Russia. Steffens recognized that this need to go to Russia was more than a professional interest. In the final analysis, he admitted to his sister that he had no better reason for the journey than "it seems to me I must be there;" he must examine this revolution "personally." In Russia, Steffens was sure that he would glimpse, at last, the "first phase" of the future. Nothing he saw during his visit belied this prediction. When Lenin took control of the revolution in late 1917, Steffens rejoiced that the "Bolsheviks are on top. . . . It's good news for Russia. They don't go back; they go on." Steffens was ready to march with them, not as a Marxist revolutionary, but as a radical American liberal.[3]

During this period, Steffens was sure that both liberal America and revolutionary Russia wanted to end the pernicious war with a just peace. For Steffens, World War I was nothing more than a destructive, monstrous act perpetrated by selfish governments: "the great war was a fight among the European conquerors to reduce the number of empires and to advance toward the decision as to which of them is finally to rule the world." While he was horrified by the effect the war effort had on American democracy, Steffens never doubted the virtues of Wilson's peace program. In "What Free Russia Asks of Her Allies," which appeared in the August 1917 issue of *Everybody's Magazine,* Steffens equated the war aims of the Russian revolutionaries with those of the American liberals. Steffens warned that the Russian people would remain in the war only to fight for "freedom and democracy for the whole world." This led Steffens to support a less than modest proposal. "The United States and Russia, the two new allies," he declared, "should demand that the war be fought out only for justice and right; not for money or territory, or empire, but for ideals." This anti-imperialistic senti-ment was only the first in a series of remarkable similarities Steffens was to discover between revolutionary Russia and liberal America.[4]

In many respects, Steffens found the Russian Revolution to be an extension of the American dream. In "Midnight In Russia," published in *McClure's* in May 1918, Steffens used a Jewish-American officer in the Red Army to teach his American audience " 'to know and to love Russia.' " In Steffens' account, this young officer visits Steffens one cold, snowy night in Moscow to tell him why he had become a revolutionary. The son of a Russian Jew, the soldier had fled czarist Russia as a boy with his father to " 'our vision of the land of promise: America.' " Instead of finding a utopia, the father and child " 'were misled, misdirected—robbed, till we had nothing. Nothing. It was an awakening—from the dream.' " At the outbreak of World War I, the young man had returned to Russia to defend his motherland and had stayed to join the revolution. As he told Steffens, he was now a revolutionary, confidently struggling to realize " 'that vision of the United States' " in Russia.[5]

This story must have both reassured and disturbed its readers. On the one hand, Steffens was placing the Russian Revolution squarely within the scope of the American political tradition. The revolution was following the path of the American experiment. According to Steffens, the Russian revolutionaries were only sharing the dream of " 'our fathers, the Puritan fathers who found and founded the American colonies.' " As Steffens explained it to the Jewish-American soldier and his American audience, the American vision had become the " 'dream of all mankind.' " Put this way, the Russian Revolution was certainly no threat to the United States. Still, this story contained a very definite tension. The Jewish-American soldier had been unable to realize the American dream in the United States. To find his " 'dream,' " he had been forced to return to Russia. This could not have been very comforting to American readers, who remained convinced that the United States was the center of democracy and progress. Yet Steffens' interest was only to take a gentle swipe at America's self-image. In the end, Steffens portrayed the revolution as little more than progressive liberalism in Russian clothing.[6]

For Steffens, the moving, governing force of the revolution was the " 'beautiful Russian people.' " As he told his readers in "What Free Russia Asks of Her Allies," he had expected to find something quite different in Russia. "The picture in my mind . . . was . . . a terrifying vision of an ignorant, brutal people hungry for food and hungry for vengeance, loose, free—free to wreck their will." To his apparent surprise, Steffens found the Russian people to be a " 'gentle beast.' " In truth, Steffens had never been worried about what he would find in Russia; his supposed suspicion was only a literary device. By claiming to be prepared to think the worst of the revolution, Steffens made his glowing description of Russia, its people, and their revolution all that much more convincing to his audience. Instead of a "nightmare," Steffens discovered "order; not government and no disorder. What I heard was—Justice; no law, but all men full of respect for all men." Without skipping a phrase, Steffens moved from admiration to commitment: "I was one of a great, strong, young people in a state of exaltation; lifted by ideals far, far above anything I have ever believed the human animal capable of in mass."[7]

The revolution rescued Steffens from a decade of frustration and disappointment. "Never again," Steffens insisted, would he "lose . . . belief in the possibilities in human nature in the mob." Here was a tacit admission by Steffens that his early enthusiasm for the Russian people and their revolution was more a renewal of old liberal beliefs than a conversion to new, revolutionary truths. His "gentle beast," stripped of its exotic verbal garb and metaphors, was not very much different from the American people as he described them in *Upbuilders:*

Uninformed and misinformed; pauperized or over-worked; misled or betrayed by their leaders—financial, industrial, political and ecclesiastical, the people are suspicious and weary and very, very busy, but they are none the less, the first, last, and best appeal in all great human cases. . . . And the reason seems to be, not that they are better than their betters, but that they are more disinterested; they are not possessed by possessions; they have not so many "things" and "friends." They can afford, they are free to be fair. And though each individual in the great crowd lacks some virtues, they all together have what no individual has, a combination of all the virtues.

Of course, the American "crowd" had failed to fulfill Steffens' expectations. Eventually, it had proved fickle and betrayed progressivism. Now Steffens was sure that the Russian "mob" would succeed where the American people had failed him.[8]

Steffens' American "crowd" and his Russian "mob" shared much in common. In 1909, he described the American people as being full of "mercy" and "forgiveness." Almost a decade later, he agreed with a friend's assessment that the Russian "mob" was the " 'rightest, gentlest, justest—safest thing I ever felt.' " In his articles, Steffens made much of the fact that the first official act of the revolutionary government had been to abolish capital punishment. He assured his American readers that with "few explainable exceptions," the Russian "mob" was a "marvel of order and dignity." Where there were isolated cases of violence, it was the likes of soldiers shooting their "brutes of officers" or the people killing policemen who, for profit, had hoarded food from the starving nation. Steffens explained that even these acts of violence were neither as common nor as "terrible" as reported by foreign observers and reporters.[9]

Such a defense of the people did not place Steffens in the ideological camp of either the liberals or the revolutionaries. At this time, American progressives as well as Marxist revolutionaries believed in "man in the mass." It was his explanation of why the Russian "mob" was so good and gentle that placed Steffens squarely, if temporarily, in the American liberal tradition. In "Midnight In Russia," Steffens argued that the Russian "mob" was so " 'right' " because it had " 'no education.' " Again, this kind of reasoning was strikingly similar to his analysis of the American "crowd" in *Upbuilders*. Like the Russian people, the American people were "wise" at least partly because they were "ignorant." After both his investigation of American reform and the initial stage of the Russian Revolution, Steffens had reached the same conclusion: somehow, the "uninformed and misinformed" masses were the best source for either reform or revolution. Steffens' "man in the mass" was much closer to being a combination of noble savage and yeoman farmer than class conscious worker.[10]

Steffens used a kind of primitive communalism or pastoralism to explain the Russian Revolution. In "The Rumor in Russia," which appeared in the December 1918 issue of *The Nation* under the pseudonym "Christian," Steffens explained how,

All witnesses testify . . . that under the yoke of generations of their servitude, the Russian people became little children. They were whipped, as children are whipped; worked as children are worked, beyond their strength and beyond their understanding. They are untaught, mistaught, misled; they are lied to. And they believed as children believe, lies and truths together. For they were kept in the dark, and they were afraid of the dark. They were kept quiet, and . . . they were kept drunk and stupid. But they could not be still. . . . Seeking, ever seeking, they groped blindly through the night for the light of a word, as children grope, restless in terror of the darkness which was about them and with them.[11]

Like children or primitives, Steffens characterized the Russian "mob" as being innocent. Although this innocence kept the Russian people in the "darkness" of ignorance, he claimed that it also prepared them for the revolution. Because they were not educated, the masses were not taught "to see wrong, and—accept wrong." In fact, Steffens insisted that quite the opposite was true. Their minds were "clean, like the baby's," and consequently, they saw the world "just as it is." Steffens carried his theory of primitivism so far as to have the Jewish-American revolutionary in "Midnight In Russia" compare the Russian "mob" with the American Indian. Like the Indians, the Russian people were "human nature in the raw" and, therefore, naturally saw the purpose of the revolution. They were not blinded by an artificial knowledge and sense of right and wrong. Yet, Steffens realized that he could not rest the revolution on the intuitive wisdom of naive children. Quickly, Steffens recognized what he felt was the essential difference between the Indians and the Russian people.[12]

To make the Russians revolutionaries, Steffens brought them out of the wilderness and into society. He claimed that, unlike the American Indians, the Russians "live and do work in communities, and they think and feel as they hold their land, as communities." Described in this manner, the Russian peasants came close to living a pastoral ideal. While innocent of the corruption caused by civilization and authority, they were not so "hopelessly free" that they had no experience of community and, therefore, no social sense. The Russian people, those "newborn men" as Steffens called them, had developed a "community sense" in their close-knit villages. For Steffens, this was the natural state of consciousness for social man. It enabled the Russian "mob" to unite as "one people" in pursuit of the common good. Obviously, Steffens was not using the term "man in the mass" in any Marxist way. What he was essentially talking about was man in the community. His "man in the mass" belonged more to liberal America than to proletarian Russia.[13]

Not surprisingly, Steffens then reduced the goals of the revolution to his own curious brand of Christian-progressive reform. According to Steffens, it was the Russian "mob," not the American "crowd," who were making "Christianity . . . practicable." He heard the Russians proclaim and saw them practice a standard of conduct even more generous than the Golden Rule: "We, the people, must not do to others any of the things that have been done to us." As a "Christian," Steffens applauded their efforts "to establish the Kingdom of Heaven here on earth, now." This "Kingdom of Heaven" had much in common with Steffens' old progressive vision for American society. In their naive, communal wisdom, the Russian people were struggling "for community success, the common good, the welfare of man." Steffens warned that the great threat to the realization of this kind of society was the development of "interests" within the community. He was happy to report to his readers that the Russian people were fully aware of this danger and wanted " 'no interest . . . that is not a common, a community interest.' "[14]

For Steffens, it was the willingness of the Russian people to use radical methods to gain their goals that marked the difference between the Russian Revolution and American progressivism. For example, to end the influence of special interests in government, American progressives had tried to remove the political barriers between the people and their representatives. To accomplish this end, these reformers, Steffens included, had supported electoral and legislative reform. The Russian Revolution carried this idea to its radical and successful conclusion. Instead of simply reforming the institutional relationship between the people and their government, the Russian people were abolishing all barriers between themselves and their leaders. From what Steffens saw during his visit, the Russian people "were rising above themselves to work out with humility and confidence, with passion, but with caution, their common—the nation's, the people's—job." Astonishingly, the Russian people were "literally" making national policy.[15]

Steffens traced this extraordinary, almost mystical ability of the Russian people to act in harmony to their communal experience. As peasants, the Russians had never known either the exercise of power or the ownership of property. According to Steffens, it was the traditional way of life for Russians to live as brothers on their communally held lands. Without fully realizing it, Steffens was providing an unique explanation for the failure of American reform and the success of the Russian Revolution. By placing the Russian people in a primitive, communal state, he was saving them from the corrupting influence of modern mores and institutions. While the American people were participating in all the social, political, economic, and intellectual movements that went into creating twentieth century society, their Russian counterparts remained socially virtuous in their pure, natural communities. In effect, Steffens had made the Russian people into revolutionaries by removing them from history.

It was little wonder that Steffens could not adequately explain why the Russian people saw the "light" of revolutionary truth in 1917. He could offer only the lamest excuses for the revolt of the Russian people against their oppressors. Thus, Steffens insisted in several articles that the prohibition of vodka was the immediate cause of the revolution. To control the innocent, communal Russian people, Steffens explained, the czar had kept the peasants " 'drunk, drunk, drunk all the time.' " When the government made the mistake of outlawing the consumption of liquor during the war, the Russian people " 'looked up, sober, clean, clear-eyed. It was an awakening; like being born at the age of eighteen or twenty-five; and it was like looking out for the first time upon the world.' " The Russian people, knowing no " 'wrong,' " then " 'naturally' " rose in revolution.[16]

The absurdity of such an argument did not disturb Steffens at all. Despite his protestations to the contrary, Steffens was not, during this period, interested in the Russian Revolution as a historic prototype. Although he insisted that he was observing the revolution with the detachment of a social scientist, Steffens was actually basing his description and analysis on long-held liberal assumptions. Neither his belief in the goodness and innocence of human nature nor his faith in the social solidarity of the pastoral, semiprimitive community took into account the fact of social change. These liberal ideals were static—timeless in their validity and their application to social reality. In traditional American liberal ideology, these concepts of human nature and community often served as part of the fixed foundation for American democracy. Like so many other liberals, Steffens used such ideals to judge the nature and character of social change. At this point, Steffens was not concerned with processes of history. For liberals, including Steffens, the inevitability of progress took care of that question.

By the end of World War I, the faith in progress was the last, strong underpinning of the whole liberal-progressive ideology. With other reformers, Steffens did not recognize that the liberal concept of progress had a basic flaw. Although he was not aware of it, Steffens was always confusing history with progress. Essentially, Steffens believed in progress—that being the continual advancement of mankind toward the realization of fixed and unchanging social ideals. For Steffens, history was the description of past progress and not the maker of the future. As a consequence, Steffens' entire early analysis of the Russian Revolution had nothing to do with the course of Russian history. When Steffens claimed that the triumph of the revolution was the victory of "human nature in the raw," he was denying that history shaped the character of the revolution. When he placed the origins of the social-political ideals of the revolution within a primitive communalism, he was making the future the product of a mythical past. In his ahistorical analysis, Steffens was dismissing the Industrial Revolution, urbanization, and the rise of the modern state as causal factors in the revolution. As a liberal, Steffens was confusing static ideals with dynamic social change, progress with history. Events were about to teach Steffens the bitter truth. [17]

In February of 1919, Steffens made his second trip to Russia and was again part of an unofficial, diplomatic delegation. This time he went with William C. Bullitt, the young, brilliant, wealthy diplomat from Main Line Philadelphia. As commissioned by the Wilson administration and the British government, the Bullitt mission was to explore the possibility of ending hostilities between the Bolsheviks and the Allies. Both the audacious Bullitt and the always hopeful Steffens made the journey, confident that they could negotiate a settlement between the two sides. When they returned to the Paris Peace Conference with what they felt was the basis for an agreement, Wilson quietly repudiated their efforts. This unexpected blow shattered Steffens' dream that liberal America and revolutionary Russia might cooperate in the building of a just peace and a better world. This, combined with what Steffens considered Wilson's overall failure at Versailles, finally broke Steffens' liberal faith. [18]

In his writings, the disillusioned Steffens made Wilson the epitome of the deficiencies of liberalism. "Woodrow Wilson was not only a well-grounded liberal of the old school of Jefferson; he was the strongest liberal whom we could have had in his place. He was liberalism personified, and when he failed, liberalism failed. And he did fail." In his *Autobiography*, Steffens used himself to demonstrate that Wilson's weaknesses were shared by all liberals. Very deliberately, Steffens emphasized his own long support of the president and his policies. When Wilson spoke the "liberal language, principles—bunk," he was speaking the lifelong language of Steffens and his fellow American reformers. After watching Clemenceau, the French realist, crush Wilson, the "righteous man," Steffens repudiated what he felt was the tragic, wrongheaded idealism of "moral American culture." [19]

Steffens spent little time ruminating over the collapse of liberalism. Instead, he quickly adopted the Russian Revolution as his new social vision and the hope of the world. In what became a celebrated rejoinder for those who criticized or doubted the Bolshevik revolution, Steffens proclaimed, " 'I have been over in the future, and it works.' " Yet, for the first time, Steffens separated his own fate from his social vision. The moment Steffens repudiated the moral culture of American liberals for the economic, scientific culture of Russian Marxists, Steffens removed himself from the future. Although he could "recognize salvation," Steffens argued that it was too late for liberals like himself to "be saved." For the remainder of his life, Steffens insisted that he and his friends, both liberals and radicals alike, were too much the products of American liberalism to be made "fit and ready" to pass over into the promised land of the Russian Revolution.[20]

This belief very much changed the way Steffens thought and wrote about the revolution. When he removed himself from the American liberal camp, he introduced a harshness into his social perspective. While Steffens had always claimed to be a realist, he had tempered his criticisms and judgments of men and society with the warmth of his humanity. Now, Steffens lost his compassion and bowed to the inevitable processes of history. A "broken liberal," Steffens could only describe and approve of the Bolshevik revolution. This attitude permitted Steffens to condone and defend some of the more brutal aspects of the revolution without feeling any sense of individual responsibility. For the first time in his career, Steffens was supporting a social-political movement that had nothing to do with him personally. Consequently, he could have it both ways. Although Steffens never joined the Communist party or the revolution, he eventually left no doubt that he accepted the judgment of history.[21]

Steffens did not change his outlook all at once. His "Report on the Bullitt Mission," published as a pamphlet after he presented it to the Senate Foreign Relations Committee in September 1919, showed him to be in transition from a liberal to a revolutionary point of view. Despite his disappointment with Wilson, Steffens found it difficult to break completely free of his old sentiments. Without much conviction, he reiterated the liberal arguments that he had developed in his earlier pieces about the revolution. The Russians, those "gentle people" as Steffens still called them, had destroyed property and lives only under the influence of alcohol. With the triumph of the revolution, prohibition became the "universal and absolute" law of the land, and the Russians then returned to their naturally peaceful ways. As Steffens himself would admit, he repeated this kind of reasoning at least partly out of habit. Yet the presentation of his original analysis of the causes and nature of the Russian Revolution served an important purpose. Steffens was setting up his old liberal self as a straw man to be discredited by the logic of the historical process.[22]

In the "Report," Steffens' more radical, almost Bolshevik, analysis of the revolution followed hard on the heels of his moderate explanation. When compared to the soft rationalizations of the liberal mentality, this new description of the revolutionary process stood out like the harsh, real truth. The destruction was caused not by the drunken mob, but by a "suppressed, betrayed . . . an almost destroyed people." Where moments before Steffens had argued that violence was the product of too much vodka, he now saw the "destructive period" of the revolution as a historical necessity used by the Communists "to destroy the old system, root, branch, fruit and blossom, too." The inevitability of the revolutionary process dominated both Steffens' vision and his style:

While the mobs broke windows, smashed wine cellars, and pillaged buildings to express their rage, their leaders directed their efforts to the annihilation of the system itself. They pulled down the Czar and his officers; they abolished the courts, which had been used to oppress them; they closed shops, . . . and took over all the great industries, monopolies, concessions, and natural resources. This was their purpose. This was their religion. This is what the lower-class culture has been slowly teaching the people of the world for fifty years; that it is not some particular evil, but the whole system of running business and railroads, shops, banks, . . . that must be changed. This is what causes poverty and riches, they teach, misery, corruption, vice, and war. The people, the workers, or their state, must own and run these things "for service."

Steffens believed that it was this irresistible revolutionary logic that most startled the world. But not Steffens; he was prepared to follow the Bolsheviks and their revolution to its implacable, scientific end.[23]

Steffens took an almost gleeful pleasure in challenging the liberal sensibilities of his American audience. Without hesitation or apology, he readily admitted the absence of democracy in revolutionary Russia. Steffens told his readers that the Russians lived under "the most autocratic government I have ever seen. Lenin, head of the Soviet government, is farther removed from the people than the

Czar." In his *Autobiography*, written in the decade after his conversion to the Marxist point of view, Steffens dismissed all criticism of the Russian Revolution based on "liberal instincts and doctrines." While he was convinced that "nothing but revolution would save us," Steffens found his erstwhile liberal colleagues still adhering to their outmoded political and social theories. When they criticized the "Red" terror, Steffens answered that it was an "inevitable" and "natural" part of the revolution. The insistence that the Bolsheviks were "too literal, too ruthless and logical," was, for Steffens, only an excuse for the failure of liberalism. In his estimation, these were the very reasons why the Communists were successfully establishing a new, egalitarian society in Russia.[24]

For Steffens, Lenin best exemplified the difference between the liberal and the true revolutionary. In his *Autobiography*, and in articles such as "The Greatest of Liberals," Steffens portrayed the Bolshevik leader as a man whose inclinations and sensibilities were, in fact, close to those of the liberal. As sketched by the admiring journalist, Lenin was an idealist, a scholar, a humanist—a man whose generous sentiments and sense of humor made him almost "too liberal" for his revolutionary duty. Nevertheless, this was the same man whose iron will and masterful leadership made possible the victory of the revolution. Despite his humanism, Steffens understood Lenin to be a "grim realist," who studied and "knew his history." This combination was what made Lenin and the Bolsheviks so different from the liberals. In his review of the memoirs of Charles Edward Russell, muckraker, liberal, and socialist journalist, Steffens argued that the liberals always suffered a fatal loss of nerve at the critical moment. While Russell was ready to perform one of his intellectual "autopsies" on the revolution in October 1917, Lenin saw that the revolution "was at the historical depth, where it must not stop and turn, but go ahead and, for once, finish—at any cost, at *any* cost." At a time when liberals such as Russell were ready to give up and begin again, Lenin "was for jamming the thing through to the bitter end." The great Bolshevik leader was the planner, not the believer, the doer, not the intellectual—the revolutionary, not the liberal.[25]

It was little wonder that Steffens let Lenin completely dominate their interview, held during the journalist's second visit to Russia. By his own account of the meeting, there was little evidence of Steffens, the tough, knowledgeable, skeptical, persistent interviewer. Instead, Steffens permitted his subject to control the conversation and to turn it into a propaganda piece for the Bolsheviks. The interview was less a discussion than a lesson taught by the Russian dictator. As Steffens described himself in his *Autobiography*, he left the meeting with the kind of excitement experienced by a student after listening to a great teacher: "When I came out of it, I found that I had fertile ideas in my mind and an attitude which grew upon me." His deference to Lenin was perfectly understandable. Steffens believed that his own lifelong adherence to liberalism disqualified him from judging the revolution. On the other hand, Lenin, the architect of the Bolsheviks' triumph, was the master of historic truth. He was a "navigator," while Steffens, like President Wilson, was only a "sailor" on the sea of history. This gave Steffens little choice but to report the revolution as the Russian dictator described it.[26]

Steffens' discovery of history turned his admiration of great men into awe. In the past, he had appreciated dominating leaders because their "intelligence," their understanding of their environment, had enabled them to control their surroundings. As a liberal, Steffens never let his respect for these powerful men interfere with his own social responsibility. Despite his admiration for such commanding figures as the urban boss and the Wall Street lawyer, Steffens harshly condemned their antisocial, antidemocratic activities even as he saw that these men could place themselves, their talents, and their knowledge at the service of society. Steffens, the disillusioned liberal, dismissed such judgments of men and their actions as being nothing more than the products of "preconceived liberal principles."

Not only did Steffens insist that strong leaders were essentially above criticism, but he developed an almost compulsive need to condone their actions. Although he was unaware of it, he confused the plans of powerful leaders with the inevitable course of events. In the case of Lenin, this did not make any difference. As the dictator of Soviet Russia, he was, according to Steffens' own analysis, in perfect harmony with history. The same could not be said of other powerful world figures, and the result was confusion. Notwithstanding his allegiance to Marxism, Steffens wanted even anti-Communist leaders to be somehow masters of their own fates. His fascination with Mussolini was a perfect example of the contradiction between his historical determinism and his admiration for strong personalities. When Mussolini asked Steffens if he had learned anything from World War I, the peace, and the Russian Revolution, he bowed to the dictator's superiority. "God's question to man, that! Could we, could I, learn from experience, from history, from events, he meant, as he could and did. Or did I stick to my principles, theories, in the face of the plain facts?" On this basis, Steffens, the apologist for Lenin and the Russian experiment, defended the leader of Italian fascism.[27]

Steffens admired more than Mussolini's sense of history. For him, the dictator epitomized the "willful man of action." He was intrigued with the "Divine Dictator" who made history serve his purposes. As Steffens analyzed his rise to power, Mussolini was able to gain control of Italy's destiny because he understood "the method, the spirit, the stuff, of Bolshevism, and used it to go—right." In effect, Steffens came perilously close to arguing that Mussolini, knowing the direction of history, could act to command its course. The fact that this contradicted the principles of historical determinism did not bother Steffens. He was apparently oblivious to this inconsistency in his writings. For example, in *The Autobiography*, he compared Mussolini with Lenin and then identified both with history without explaining how two such diametrically opposed leaders could both be in step with the irresistible course of events.

But Mussolini's power and his triumph came . . . from his faith, his scientific confidence, in facts and in history. Like Lenin. These new, revolutionary leaders read history, and not as scholars do, for love of a growing body of knowledge, not even as scientists seeking the laws that govern events, but as men of action, reading a record of human experimentation to find out what can be done and how. They detect, they think, the workings of elementary forces, and they hitch their wagon to these—not to stars, but to historically discovered and experimentally proved going concerns. They don't judge men and events; they try to understand them to prophesy and steer by. History, both current and classic, told Mussolini that he was historically due—he and Lenin.

In the end, Steffens fell back on a resigned fatalism for a defense of his position. Everyone was caught in the current of history. The difference was that Mussolini and Lenin knew their destinations, while the rest, including Steffens, blindly rode the waves of change.[28]

Since Steffens felt that it was too late for him to join the forefront of history, he confined himself to the task of explaining and supporting the revolution. Shortly after his second visit to Russia, he conceived the idea of writing a parable to explain the inexorable pattern of revolutions. Long fascinated with the figure of Moses, Steffens chose the exodus of the Jews from Egypt to serve as his story line. It took him approximately six years to turn this idea into a polished manuscript. In good part, this long delay was caused by his lingering doubts about the Russian experiment. It was only after Steffens made his third and final visit to the Soviet Union in 1923 that he was able to dispel these reservations. Finally published in 1926, *Moses In Red* is Steffens' most complete defense of the Russian revolution.[29]

Steffens insisted that *Moses In Red* was not just about the Bolshevik revolution. His parable about the flight of the children of Israel under the leadership of Moses was, as far as Steffens was concerned, the story of all revolutions. He believed that revolutions were inevitable consequences of human interference in social evolution. In his introduction to the book, he defined revolution as a "natural phenomenon, as natural and as understandable as a flood, a fire, or a war . . . an epidemic of disease, or a pimple on the nose. It has its causes and its natural history." This made it possible for Steffens, the self-proclaimed scientific observer, to discover and analyze the natural laws that governed each and every revolution. He even held out some hope that this knowledge might make revolutions "preventable" by eliminating the impediments to "evolution" that caused them. This proved to be no easy out for those trying to avoid the consequences of a revolution. Steffens simply meant that the alternative to revolution was full and immediate support of the goals of the revolution.[30]

This was clear from his carefully calculated choice of a story from the Old Testament. In the first chapter of *Moses In Red*, "The Point of View," Steffens established how the Bible offered him a unique social perspective. He had first discovered this during his investigations of American corruption and reform. Quite by accident, Steffens had found a striking similarity between the life of Jesus as it was told in the New Testament and the careers of such reformers as Judge Ben Lindsey and Tom Johnson. Like Jesus, these progressive leaders offered reform based on "love and understanding," but were rejected by the "righteous" citizens of society. This led Steffens to reject reform and the New Testament and to embrace the need for revolution and the lessons of the Old Testament. Obviously, Steffens was using the Bible to show how he had changed his own social perspective—his point of view. As a reformer, he had asked all citizens, including the righteous, to accept the gentle, loving Christ. As a student of revolution, he was making these same righteous people face the implacable Jehovah of history.[31]

Surely, Steffens realized that there was little difference between the point of view of the righteous and that of the revolutionary. Both judged men and events with their own kind of uncompromising certitude. For Steffens, the historical determinist, there was no appeal against the necessity of the natural laws that shaped human conduct. Using this as the basis for his criticisms, Steffens turned *Moses In Red* into a harsh, almost unrelenting attack on liberalism. He began by dismissing the liberal's faith in democratic government. In its place, he offered the "general law" that the dictatorship was the *"first, the simplest and perhaps the best form of government."* From his supposedly dispassionate observations, Steffens had learned that dictators were the only ones who could bring order and direction to societies caught in crisis. Accordingly, he reasoned that the belief that men valued liberty first and foremost was only the product of *"man-made laws and soul-felt idealism."* In fact, history showed that the "natural law" contradicted the ideals of democracy. Men sought security and then, having secured it, granted freedom.[32]

For all the boldness of his attack on liberal values, Steffens could not bring himself to denounce overtly his own long-held liberal faith in the wisdom of the people. He left the repudiation of this belief in the virtuous, collective citizenry to the parable itself. This indirect approach was markedly different from the usual format Steffens used to reject liberal values in *Moses In Red*. In other cases, he refuted a liberal principle with the general laws of nature and then made the parable support his point. With the ideal of the people, he forced the symbolism of the Old Testament story to carry the whole burden of his criticism. In Steffens' scheme, the exodus from Egypt represents the "typical revolution," and the children of Israel personify "the people—any people." The Jews do not resemble, in any manner or form, the "wise . . . mass of man" of *Upbuilders* or even the "gentle beast" of his early essays about the Russian Revolution.[33]

In the parable, the people are not the strength of the revolution, but rather the "chief difficulty" blocking its success. The children of Israel, the people, are incapable of seizing their freedom, but have it pushed upon them by the pharaoh. As the symbol of the old order, the pharaoh is the "indispensible force" that makes the timid Israelites give up their bonds. This was not a new argument on the

part of Steffens. He had long contended that a reactionary government inevitably caused its own overthrow with its repressive
measures. Steffens used this story to make a significantly different
point. He was not only maintaining that the Egyptian ruler caused
the people to revolt, a truism in Marxist doctrine, but that he was
responsible for their success. In Steffens' revolutionary parable, the
children of Israel never lose their "disposition to return to . . . their
chains." At no point do the people develop a class consciousness.
Instead, it is only the retributive efforts of the pharaoh that prevent
the people from embracing their old bondage. Even after they are
free of the old regime, the Israelites are not ready for the promised
land—Steffens' symbol for a revolutionary society. Again and again,
the people falter, and Moses, the revolutionary dictator, is forced to
implement the bloodiest kind of terror to keep them on the correct
path toward the promised land. By the end of the story, it is obvious
that even this is fruitless and that the future is reserved for the
"unspoiled, the untaught, the unformed" next generation.[34]

The overall tone of *Moses In Red* is one of dark pessimism. The
book is strewn with the wreckage of liberal principles and ideals,
with little mention or praise of positive aspects of the revolution. In
fact, Steffens wrote *Moses In Red* more as a disillusioned liberal
than as a devoted revolutionary. This was in keeping with Steffens'
own accurate image of himself as a "broken liberal" who wholeheartedly supported the Russian Revolution. He never claimed to
be a Marxist ideologue. Consequently, his defense of the Bolshevik
Revolution had a negative quality. In *Moses In Red*, Steffens did
not entreat his readers to support or join the Communists. Readily
admitting the "tragedy" and "horror" of a revolution, he only asked that they understand the inevitability of the revolutionary
process. Regrettably, the terror, both red and white, was a natural
phenomenon that "always" accompanied a revolution. For Steffens,
the only hope for man was to learn the "divine truth as God reveals
it to us in nature." With such knowledge, there was at least the
possibility that the people might bloodlessly and peacefully reach
their historic, shared destiny.[35]

However, *Moses In Red* does not support even this dim hope. As
created by Steffens, Moses himself, the revolutionary leader, is little
more than a passive tragic figure. The dominant character in the
parable is Jehovah, who represents nature. Jehovah is the master of
the revolutionary process, and Moses is his servant. Steffens
appeared to be taking his revenge on Lenin for reducing him to be-

ing a spectator of history. He made Moses—Lenin—follow the plan of nature and did not give him either the satisfaction of saving his people or of entering the promised land. In *Moses In Red*, Steffens reduced the revolutionary leader to being as unworthy of the future as any unredeemable liberal. In fact, the dictator's vision of the promised land proved to be no more possible than Steffens' old liberal dream. "Moses' land of promise was a place of the imagination. . . . It must have been beautiful beyond compare; free, fair, and—finished. No real country could possibly be so perfect." Ironically, Steffens' model revolutionary leader had no more ability to see, much less shape, the future than the most unscientific of liberals.[36]

This, of course, was in sharp contrast to much of what he wrote concerning revolutionary leaders. He was ambiguous about the role of strong men in the revolutionary process from his essays on Mexico until his death. In his study of the Mexican revolution, Steffens consistently described leaders such as Carranza as servants of events. This was easy to do with Mexico, which had no dynamic figure dominating its revolution. The emphasis was different with Lenin and Mussolini. In their cases, Steffens often blurred the relationship between their decisive leadership and the direction of history. Steffens felt more comfortable giving men credit for change, and these leaders provided him with the opportunity to put men back at the center of the action. When, on the other hand, the movement of history became the focus of his writing, Steffens lost his enthusiasm. His vision of the future became darker, and there was less place for the willful man of action.

Until *Moses In Red*, Steffens had always insisted that the scientific study of human activity was the essential basis for progress. Social advancement was no more than a combination of such knowledge with motivation and correct purpose. This was premised on his belief that all men had a "common, controllable fate"—the basis for much of his exuberance for life. As a public man, Steffens wanted to take part in the planning, announcing, and managing of a bright future. In *Moses In Red*, he denied that this was possible even for the Bolsheviks. He now felt that science could not serve as a guide to help man shape malleable nature. Such information was only a map that helpless man might use to plot the inevitable course of history. *Moses In Red* is Steffens' cheerless acceptance of this fate for both himself and mankind. Fortunately, Steffens was finding solace and joy not in his public career, but in his private life.[37]

CHAPTER 8

A Life Worth Writing

A T the very time Steffens' career was going into steep, apparently irreversible, decline, his private life was taking a definite turn for the better. In April 1919, Steffens met Ella Winter, a student at the London School of Economics who was serving as an aid to Felix Frankfurter at the Paris Peace Conference. Bright, articulate, energetic, and idealistic, she was everything that Steffens admired in youth. The worldly wise journalist was soon guiding his young friend around Paris and through the maze of intrigue and politics that was the peace conference. Despite numerous obstacles, not the least of which was the great difference in their ages, they quickly developed a deep affection for each other. After several attempts by Steffens to end their relationship, they finally decided to marry in 1924. To his great surprise (Steffens was in his fifties and his first marriage had been barren) and joy, he quickly became a father. Peter Stanley Steffens was born in November of 1924. After some fleeting misgivings, Steffens settled into his position as father and responsible family man. At an age when most men look forward to retirement, Steffens was beginning a whole new life.[1]

Fatherhood immediately and deeply affected Steffens' art as well as his life. From the birth of Peter to his own death a dozen years later, Steffens wrote numerous articles and essays describing and philosophizing about the experience of being a parent. In "Radiant Fatherhood," written within a year of his son's birth, Steffens recalled the emotions and feelings of becoming a parent for the first and, in his case, only time. From the moment he heard of his wife's pregnancy, Steffens realized that he had wanted a child "all my life." During the delivery, Steffens stood helplessly by and watched the doctor and his nurse turn this beautiful event into a "hateful, dominating, efficient thing" with their cool, detached professionalism. Such observations put Steffens some fifty years ahead of his time. Yet Steffens was not above the most traditional

118

expressions of fatherly pride. Unashamedly, he announced to all that would listen that his child was the "greatest baby on earth." This, he felt, was the only "sane and sensible" attitude for any new father.[2]

Although written during the same period, the tone of these essays is markedly different from that of his political tracts. The latter are cold, often harsh attacks on Steffens' political foes. They contain none of the warm, generous optimism expressed in his discussions of his private life. These differences are more than a matter of style and subject matter. Essentially, Steffens was separating his public from his private perspective. As a defender of the Russian Revolution, Steffens accepted the inevitability of the historical process. There was no room for flexibility or sympathy in this political philosophy; one either supported the immutable laws of social change or became their victim. In his personal life, Steffens wanted the opposite to be true. At the conclusion of "Radiant Fatherhood," he pledged to leave Peter a "fine fellow, who, whether he is a poet or a politician, a businessman, a reporter or a lounge lizard, can play the game and win, without believing in it or in his own lies." Despite the cynical edge to his promise, Steffens saw an infinite number of possibilities for his son. As a father, he believed that it was his duty to keep open these choices for Peter.[3]

In his tribute to John Reed, first published shortly after his friend's untimely death in Russia, Steffens drew a sharp distinction between his personal and his political philosophies. In his opinion, John Reed, fresh from Harvard, came as close as humanly possible to being "pure joy." As Reed's companion and surrogate father, Steffens "tried to steer him away from convictions, that he might play . . . with life; and see it all, love it all, live it all." In the end, he failed in this mission. Reed lost his carefree attitude, gained "conviction," and became a dedicated revolutionary. At this point, the author changed the tone of the essay dramatically. While Steffens made his admiration for his revolutionary friend obvious, there is no warmth in his tribute. As Steffens put it, the young, happy poet had lost his "smile." In his place was John Reed, the Communist, "hard, intolerant, ruthless, clinched for the fight." He had sacrificed his humanity in the service of the revolution. Steffens was determined to save his son from such a fate.[4]

At the same time that he was rejecting liberal politics, Steffens was embracing—as was so fashionable among American intellectuals in the 1920s—liberal or progressive theories of child raising and education. In such articles as "Becoming a Father at Sixty Is a Liberal Education," he chronicled his efforts to free Peter from what he characterized as the restrictive, traditional family unit. In a sense, Steffens wanted to liberate his son from society and history. This was liberalism with a vengeance. First, he simply dismissed the accepted familial arrangement as being unsound. He had little patience with the traditional male role in the family. Steffens skillfully argued that the common assumption that fathers were only a "hinderance" in child raising was "pure bunk." Instead of enjoying the pleasures of their children, young fathers were always off earning their fame and fortunes. Age, according to Steffens, had saved him from such foolish vanity. By becoming a parent so late in life, he was not distracted by dreams of personal glory. Consequently, he was "free enough and wise enough to enjoy [being] . . . a father, a grandfather, and a mother all in one." Steffens, then, stayed where he thought a good and fortunate father belonged—at home.[5]

Steffens believed that the problem with the traditional role of the father went far beyond his absence from the family. In good part, the difficulty was not that the adult male was so much out in the world, but that he brought the world home with him. For Steffens, the father embodied the demands that society made on the child. It was in this role as patriarch that the father stifled the creativity and spontaneity of his children. As the representative of the "grown up" world, the father taught his offspring to conform in both thought and habit to the ways of the world. Like so many other progressive parents, Steffens considered the Victorian father to be the repressive agent of social control. He forced his own father, a remarkably sensitive man by Steffens' own account, to fit into his oversimplified, mythical image of the authoritarian parent. Steffens recalled how his father took for granted his and society's infallibility and "got himself somehow into the awkward position of authority." As a result, the position of the father and the demands of society became inseparable. Each depended on the willingness of the child to accept the practiced ways of seeing and knowing the world.[6]

By describing his own relationship with Peter, Steffens hoped to show his readers how to break the repressive link between the father and society. To begin with, he refused to play the part of the omniscient, omnipotent father. In an apparent sweeping reversal of roles, Steffens let his wife "provide the science and the business side of my child's up-bringing." Without suggesting that it was in any way a compliment, Steffens claimed that Ella must take all the responsibility for making their child "a strong, knowing, successful man." For his part, he was cultivating what was considered the mother's job in the family. While his wife was representing the authority of society, he was furnishing the "love" to his son.[7]

Steffens insisted that this unorthodox method of raising his boy was both necessary and natural. For Steffens, each generation was more physically and socially advanced than the preceding one. As a member of the newest generation, Peter was no exception. His son was the "latest and therefore, biologically the most advanced human being on earth." As such, he had a natural sociability that should be the envy of every adult. After watching Peter for several years, his proud father observed that "he has courtesy, and he has humor. He had these gifts from the very beginning and a little inquiry among other parents seems to justify me in my theory that human beings are born with good will rather than subordination, and that they are governable, from infancy up, much more gently than we think." Steffens saw that his task was to introduce his son into the world without destroying his innate social superiority. This meant not only protecting these delicate, natural virtues with motherly love, but also nurturing them with respect.[8]

By treating his son as a friend and "equal," Steffens encouraged the development of Peter's natural dignity. This was typical of avant-garde thought in the 1920s, and it never occurred to him that love and attention could be just as oppressive as discipline and authority. In "Becoming a Father at Sixty Is a Liberal Education," he described, rather melodramatically, the challenge of his egalitarian approach to child raising. When his son refused to obey his admonishments that he quit sucking his thumb, Steffens realized that "my prestige, my authority, my place at the head of the family were at stake, and I was frightened." Despite his fear, Steffens did not resort to demanding unthinking obedience from his child. Instead, he made use of Peter's natural politeness and playfulness to obtain the desired result. Steffens stopped the thumb sucking by making the cure into a humorous game. In other cases, the attentive father found that his son inevitably responded to any "reasonable" and "courteously" made request. Such reactions only reaffirmed his "deep faith in the [intellectual] courtesy and a high hope in the inborn capacity of our successors—youth."[9]

For Steffens, preserving and encouraging his son's independence within the family was only half the battle. Peter still had to face a

society that would try to close off his creative instincts. No matter
what the faults of the world, "grown ups" were always falsely insisting that everything was fine and perfect. This led to an early
"process of mind-fixing and standardization" that made the young
old before their time. It was this, according to Steffens, that caused
the world to go wrong and ruined the young. He was determined to
expose society before his son learned to trust its judgments. Steffens
began with himself. At the first opportunity, he admitted to Peter
that he had few, if any of the answers. When they played games,
Steffens fixed it so that his son was, more often than not, the
winner. In this manner, he gave Peter a "superiority complex." As
for the world, Steffens taught his son "*that nothing is done, finally
and completely.*" With this mind, he advised his son to avoid the illusions of certainty but, at the same time, to remember that "the
future is sunny and wonderful."[10]

Steffens hoped to guarantee his son a bright or, at least, financial-
ly secure future with the royalties from his *Autobiography*. Since
Peter was instrumental in the writing of the book, it was altogether
fitting that he reap the economic benefit of its sale. Even as he
began the *Autobiography*, Steffens admitted that Peter was making
"my book possible and purposeful." As he watched his son grow
and change, Steffens remembered his own childhood, his parents,
and his home in California. Steffens, with his son to inspire him,
wrote quickly without revisions. "I am not rewriting; I go straight
on," he told Maria Howe, a close friend and sympathetic editor. He
found these first chapters about his early life to be "a great joke, a
sport, a play." Things went smoothly until he reached the section
about his first wife, Josephine. Then for long, frustrating periods of
time, there was nothing "but rejected shreds of paper."[11]

The fun had gone out of it. For the next four years, Steffens
plodded along in fits and starts, writing his story, one that was often
painful to recreate on paper. As he struggled to recapture his past,
he tired of Europe and longed for home. In 1928 after almost a
decade of living in France and Italy, he returned to the United
States and settled in Carmel, California, the site of a new artist
colony on the Pacific coast. There, with the encouragement of his
wife, his friends, and especially his publisher, Alfred Harcourt, he
managed to complete the lengthy manuscript. Finally done with
what had become a tedious project, Steffens relaxed and decided
upon such minor details as the title. Although the author favored his
original choice, " 'My Life of Unlearning,' " he settled for the more

standard title, *The Autobiography of Lincoln Steffens*. The two volume work was published in April 1931 and was greeted, as Steffens' boasted, with a "shout of acclamation" from the critics. He proudly announced to his mother-in-law that "the publisher says the book will go on selling for a generation; as a sort of classic of our day." This is an accurate but too modest estimation of *The Autobiography*.[12]

As an essay about his life and times, *The Autobiography* continues to make fascinating reading. Here was a man who grew up in the America of the Golden West and genuine cowboys and Indians. Steffens recaptured his childhood so well that the first section of *The Autobiography*, entitled "A Boy on Horseback," was later published as a separate volume. Steffens wrote these chapters with a simple directness that reflected the uncomplicated life of growing up in Sacramento, California, in the late nineteenth century. With few exceptions, "A Boy on Horseback" has none of the moral asides and judgments that characterize the rest of the volumes. On the contrary, Steffens filled this section with the "sweetness" and "beauty" with which he recalled his happy, adventuresome childhood. Steffens had decided not to interpret the "wondering mentality of that age" but to save that kind of analysis for his later, more complicated years.[13]

The first section is in sharp contrast to the remainder of *The Autobiography*. While Steffens grew up in the comforting simplicity of nineteenth century rural, Protestant America, he made his fame and fortune in the bustling, complex, industrial, urban nation of this century. This was a disturbing but familiar change to millions of Americans, and Steffens managed to capture the ambiguity of their feelings in his *Autobiography*. On the one hand, they shared the author's sense of loss and "A Boy on Horseback" typified their common, often nostalgic memory of the past. At the same time, they recognized that modern society offered untold opportunity to those who would seize it. Faced with a choice between two kinds of America, they, like Steffens, stayed in the city and hustled. In *The Autobiography*, Steffens' childhood becomes an idyllic vision of that older, purer American that could be used by Steffens and his audience to measure, silently, the cost of that decision.

In this rapidly changing world, Steffens seemed to have known everyone and have done everything. In brilliant vignettes, almost short stories, Steffens introduced his readers to many of the important, often legendary, figures of his generation. There is J. Pierpont Morgan sitting in his open, unguarded office, protected from interruption only by his terrible temper and awesome reputation. The reader finds Steffens teaching Theodore Roosevelt how to tell a lie as the truth, playing cultural radical with John Reed in Greenwich Village, and advising Woodrow Wilson on the dangers of the president's Mexican policy. Certainly, his fame as a journalist and muckraker gave Steffens such opportunities. Just as importantly, he lived in New York for much of his career. During his lifetime, that city was the undisputed American center for the arts, finance, culture, publishing, and the entry point for European ideas and politics into the United States. The second section of *The Autobiography*, "Seeing New York First," reveals why this city proved irresistible to the young, the talented, and the bold. It was where men like Steffens started for the top and where they stayed once they got there.

Still, New York alone could not explain the stunning diversity of Steffens' friendships. Ironically, this was made possible by the very moralistic, liberal culture that Steffens was supposedly trying to bury with his life story. Americans born and raised in this nineteenth century milieu shared the feeling that all men wanted, or should want, essentially the same things for themselves and their society. In politics as well as in the arts, there was a common belief that each individual sought the best. This expressed itself as a sense of responsibility for the general improvement of one's craft or profession and for the progress of the nation. It gave American society its unity and basis for communication. No matter how men differed in profession, philosophy, and even politics, they remained in agreement about the nature of their social responsibility. Consequently, they met, exchanged views, disagreed, and established friendships in full appreciation of this commonality of purpose.[14]

The Autobiography is a fitting testimonial to the unity and generosity of this liberal culture. By Steffens' own admission, his always changing and increasingly radical views and activities seldom, if ever, cost him a friend or kept him from making new and interesting acquaintances. Steffens himself was ready to think the best of people no matter how much he disagreed with them. He was sure that, given knowledge and opportunity, criminals, urban bosses, and even big businessmen would willingly serve the public good. Although *The Autobiography* is a vigorous repudiation of liberalism, it is not a vitriolic personal attack on its standardbearers.

The "Life" treats Woodrow Wilson as a tragic figure rather than as a villain. What Steffens wrote about muckrakers and muckraking epitomized his attitude. "Those were innocent days; we were all innocent folk; but no doubt all movements, whether for good or evil, are as innocent of intentions as ours." He tempered his criticism with warmth and condemned no one for the failures of reform. Thus, in the very act of denunciation, Steffens expressed and reaffirmed, perhaps unwittingly, what many think to be the saving grace of American liberalism.[15]

However, *The Autobiography* is more than a chronicle of the author's experiences in that fascinating and rapidly changing world. It is his very personal effort to make sense of his life in those hectic times. Yet the book is less than a confession. Steffens considered that kind of public self-examination distasteful. While writing the first chapters of his own story, he had read Frederic Howe's autobiography, *The Confessions of a Reformer,* which he found much to his liking. As Steffens told its author, who was his longtime friend, "it's an honest man's story, honestly told, and I think that they have had enough of personal (psychological, sex) confessions and are relieved to find an autobiography which reveals the world; not the author, except as a hero." This was the very perspective Steffens wanted in his own book. He was interested in "showing up the world and not me."[16]

Nevertheless, Steffens did not reach this decision easily. In debates with friends about the format of the book, he wavered back and forth about the merits of including his personal or "inside" story. First of all, he argued that no one even expected him to have worthwhile observations or opinions about the intimate aspects of life. Anyway, Steffens doubted that he had either the insight or the talent to write about such matters. His own judgment that he lacked facility at this sort of writing was correct. In the few chapters of *The Autobiography* where Steffens discussed what he called the "natural life," his style is awkward and his presentation clumsy. His description of his first encounter with sex reflects the discomfort of the author with such topics. Steffens hurried through the episode without pausing to examine its importance or meaning; indeed, it is impossible for the reader to tell what actually occurred. It is little wonder that Steffens felt safer talking about his public self.[17]

Even his wives receive an "outside" treatment in *The Autobiography.* At first, Steffens planned to exclude them completely from the story. Since his wives played "no part in the development of my discovery of the world," he explained to Frederic Howe, they had no place in a book devoted to that single theme. In the end, Steffens found it impossible to eliminate them, but he did severely limit their presence. Inevitably, they appear as aspects of his relationship with society. Josephine is his conscience during their long, barren marriage. In the chapter, "Muckraking Myself—A Little," she makes her husband look at his own egotistical ambitions and the vanity of his career. After her death, Steffens discovered her diary, which portrayed him as a husband "who is thinking always of graft or business or—something else; who is always at hand but never at home." In short, Steffens was a man with little, if any, meaningful private life. All this changed with his marriage to Ella Winter and the birth of Peter. But Ella's role in *The Autobiography* is essentially one of companion in the quest for social truth, not wife and mother.[18]

Steffens recognized that this intense focus on what he called his "outside" life could be regarded as a substantial weakness by the critics. Without an extensive discussion of his private self, Steffens feared that his "life" would lack both balance and drama. His concern about this emphasis on his exterior life at the expense of his interior feelings was, in many respects, a modern contrivance. In the nineteenth century, an individual's exterior life was thought to reflect his or her interior state. An alteration in a person's relationship with the world evidenced a change in psychological condition and vice versa. An autobiography, more often than not, was a description of the author's social consciousness or recognition of a moral imperative. Public testimonials, especially political and religious ones, were expressions of the person's innermost feelings. After World War I, such essentially nineteenth century figures as Henry Adams and William Allen White continued this literary tradition with their autobiographical works. This is the format of *The Autobiography*, that appeared in print midway between Adams' *The Education of Henry Adams* and White's *The Autobiography of William Allen White*. Although Steffens understood the demands of modern literature, he could not bring himself to write a probing self-examination of his pysche. Instead, he wrote an autobiography that used his public life to reveal the social side of the private man.

Steffens' life story is a classic tale of American innocence and optimism. As usual, Steffens chose to develop his ideas in a paradoxical fashion. For many readers, *The Autobiography* seems to have quite the opposite theme; it appears to be a touching story of lost innocence and subsequent disillusionment. Steffens supplied plenty of evidence to support this contention. As the author described his life, it was a series of lost hopes and unfulfilled dreams. In the course of his career, he embraced and abandoned genteel Republican reform, muckraking, progressivism, and Christian anarchism. Finally, Steffens lost all faith in American liberalism, which had once formed the very core of his social-political perspective. By the conclusion of *The Autobiography*, Steffens had apparently given up the moral idealism of discredited liberalism for the inevitability of historical materialism. Although correct in every detail, this synopsis misses the real point of the book. [19]

The Autobiography is far from being a chronicle of disillusionment. Admittedly, it is the tale of lost illusions, but that is not the same thing. According to Steffens, he spent much of his life "unlearning" what he thought was certain and right. These discoveries did not leave him bitter and cynical. Quite the contrary was true. Early in his career, Steffens realized that "it was as pleasant to change one's mind as it was to change one's clothes. The practice led one to other, more fascinating—theories." In essence, he was never disillusioned; he simply lost his illusions over and over again. For this reason, Steffens had little patience with those liberals who let Wilson's failure at Versailles drive them to political despair. Instead of developing a new revolutionary social vision to take the place of liberalism, these disillusioned radicals satisfied themselves with "bitterness, cynicism, drink, sex—aplenty." Steffens saw no need to follow this "subjective" course. For him, the repudiation of once held principles cleared the way for new ideals and led to a reaffirmation of his social optimism. [20]

No doubt, this attitude is not the product of naivete. Certainly, Steffens willingly accepted, even romanticized, this kind of innocence. He devoted a good portion of *The Autobiography* to his unsophisticated, protected childhood in semifrontier California and his discovery of the wordly wisdom of Europe and the raw excitement of New York. In this Jamesian sense of American innocence, such a life should have led to disillusionment. American writers have often used this concept of innocence either to accept or reject what has been essentially a European claim to superiority. Although Steffens believed in the special virtues of this kind of pristine innocence, he was unwilling to identify experience with disillusionment. As much as anyone of his generation, Steffens knew the world, its people, and its leaders. While he admitted that these experiences opened his simple, Western eyes, he never conceded that they caused him to lose hope for himself and society. Throughout his life, he approached each new adventure with the same fresh anticipation of his boyhood days in California.

In *The Autobiography*, innocence is, in its fullest sense, the disposition to combine experience with fresh hope. It is more than a willingness to confront men, institutions, and ideas without the prejudice of previous disappointments. Innocence is the psychological capacity to make new experiences the efficacious basis for an ever-changing but always optimistic system of beliefs. This is not the innocence of true believers who let the righteousness of their faith cut them off from the reality of the world. Such innocence had led to the failure of liberalism. To the readers of *The Autobiography*, Steffens "offered the old rule of my experience; to look at facts, let them destroy an illusion, and not to be cast down, but go on studying the facts, sure that in those very same facts would be found constructive material with which to build up another—illusion, no better, perhaps, but other than the old one." Thus, experience never ended with cynicism, but always became the foundation for new beliefs.[21]

According to Steffens, it was his application of the objective methods of science that made possible this continued renewal of confidence that man could solve his problems. Yet, Steffens used science in an unusual way. Despite his claims to the contrary, he employed science not so much to create new theories as to destroy old ones. In *The Autobiography*, the examination of facts and experience inevitably led to the loss of belief. Steffens used the detached methodology of science to clear away principles, assumptions, ideas, and moral standards. In this way, he lost his faith in good men, good government, reform, progressivism, formal Christianity, and, of course, liberalism. From his boyhood to the moment he completed *The Autobiography*, Steffens saw the same pattern to his life. Discarded principles were quickly, almost effortlessly, replaced by other theories and ideals. For this reason, he thought the best title for his life story would be "My Life of Unlearning."[22]

The Autobiography proves Steffens to be anything but a social scientist. He showed none of the respect for facts so essential to the methods of science. What Steffens said about his analysis of the Russian Revolution can just as easily be applied to his account of his life. "I lay, not the history, but my history. . . . It is not the truth; it is my compact version of some truth and some lies that counted like facts." He was not interested in arranging the events of his life in such an objective manner that the disinterested reader might judge him and his activities. For Steffens, as always, the facts were of no consequence in and by themselves. He included only those events and occurrences in *The Autobiography* that served to shape and illuminate his social-political consciousness. He began the last chapter with the observation that "seeing is one motion; believing is another." His ability to combine the two without sacrificing the virtues of either was central to his special kind of innocence.[23]

In this respect, *The Autobiography* is less Steffens' life story than it is a reaffirmation of his faith in the world. In fact, he used the book to support his latest cause. He reiterated his by then well-known belief that the Russian experiment was the wave of the future. Still, *The Autobiography* is dominated by the "boy on horseback" and not by the hardened, unforgiving defender of the revolution. For Steffens, the young were the best hope of social redemption. They, unfettered by false knowledge and values, saw the open-ended possibilities of life. The youth of the United States, Russia, Mexico, and even Italy were making their systems work. Finally, to his surprise, he found cause for optimism in his native land. The managers had replaced the owners as the decisionmakers in society. He viewed these technocrats as planning the economy efficiently for the maximum good of all, not as manipulating the market for the outdated motive of profit. For all his apparent certainty, Steffens appreciated the irony of his latest convictions. Beliefs, by their very nature, were necessary but fleeting things, and this willing believer was sure that he would again change his mind. He finished *The Autobiography* with this thought. "My life was worth my living. And as for the world in general, all that was or is or ever will be wrong with that is my—our thinking about it."[24]

Steffens continued to think and write about himself and the world until his death in August 1936. Despite the success of *The Autobiography* and the clamor for a sequel, Steffens never again undertook a major piece of writing. In one way or another, *The Autobiography* contained all the books, either fact or fiction, that he had ever considered writing. In any case, the aging journalist was tired and wanted to relax and enjoy his new eminence in both American letters and radical politics. He went on the lecture circuit and was a great success until failing health forced him to return

home to California. Even then, Steffens managed to keep his name
in print. He wrote a few articles for such major national magazines
as *Cosmopolitan,* but mostly he contributed to leftist periodicals
and local California newspapers. Shortly before his death, Steffens
gathered much of this material into one last volume, *Lincoln
Steffens Speaking.*[25]

More often than not, these articles, essays, fables, and vignettes
concerned American capitalism and politics, their failure in the
Great Depression, and the alternative offered by communism.
Steffens' faith in the "new" capitalism did not last beyond the initial stages of the Depression. When the American economy collapsed suddenly in late 1929, Steffens expected the managers of industry to bring back prosperity by maintaining high wages and full
employment. When businessmen began firing workers and cutting
production to save expenditures and create scarcities, Steffens lost
all confidence in the ability of capitalism to reform itself. From the
start, he was sure that the reform program of the New Deal was
doomed to failure. For him, "President Roosevelt's policy of
proceeding by evolution to adjust the institutions and machinery of
the United States to change will not be possible." This meant,
Steffens concluded, that America must look to Russia and communism for the answers.[26]

During the final years of his life, Steffens became an ever more
vocal defender of the Soviet Union and outspoken advocate of communism at home. He lost all tolerance for criticism of Soviet policy.
Steffens insisted that the Russian ruler had no choice but to suppress the privileged classes with the terror in the early 1930s. While,
admittedly, this was done at "great cost," it was the only way to end
internal opposition to the Russian "social experiment." In fact,
Steffens claimed that the Communists, especially Stalin, had
become so generous—liberal—with their enemies as to encourage
resistance to their programs. This forced Stalin to reinstitute the
terror to protect the revolution. This was an imaginative, if inac-
curate, explanation of the first phase of the Russian dictator's
massive purges of the peasants, the party, and finally, the army. At
home, Steffens encouraged all radical and dissident elements to un-
ify under the Communist party. Only with the leadership of the
Communists could Americans understand their economic problems
and proceed to their permanent solution.[27]

Yet for someone who had seen the future, he remained unsure of
its shape. If life had taught him anything, Steffens told his youthful

readers, it was *"that nothing is known positively and completely."*
This is the message that he has passed on through his writing to
every generation of Americans in this century. It was the way that
he lived his life with expectations that made him a great journalist.
His continual need to see and believe in the world made it
obligatory that he be involved in the world. He was always ready to
share each experience and every discovery with his audience.
Consequently, he never tired of the ever-changing world; his outlook remained optimistic, and his prose crisp and fresh. In this
sense, his writing was indistinguishable from his life, and both exemplified the kind of American innocence that saw the frontier as a
metaphor for a willingness to confront new experiences with the optimism of a believer.[28]

In a word, Steffens was a great journalist. He was not a great
writer or thinker. He influenced the attitude of those who knew him
and not their style or thought. His two most famous proteges,
Walter Lippman and John Reed, ended having little in common
with their mentor except that they, too, became great journalists.
Today, Steffens remains a model for investigative reporting. He was
the first to understand and master this peculiarly American art.
Steffens realized that the exposure of misdeeds was not enough for
Americans. Like Steffens, they wanted the "shameful" facts
destroyed. When Steffens equated the knowledge of wrongdoing
with a demand for reform, he was speaking the language of his
audience. Modern investigative reporting is founded on the special
American virtue of seeing public wrong as the opportunity for the
general good. In this century, it is a story as old as *The Shame of the
Cities* and as new as Watergate.

Notes and References

Chapter One

1. *The Autobiography of Lincoln Steffens* (New York: Harcourt, Brace and Company, 1931), 1: 169.
2. *Ibid.*, 1: 30 - 170.
3. "A Dismal Holiday," 1900 (unpublished), Lincoln Steffens Collection, Columbia University Library, New York, New York.
4. "Hon. Frank Ditson," written before 1891 (unpublished), Steffens Collection.
5. Justin Kaplan, *Lincoln Steffens: a Biography* (New York: Simon and Schuster, 1974), p. 63.
6. *Autobiography*, 1: 180.
7. Russell Horton, *Lincoln Steffens* (New York: Twayne Publishers, 1974), pp. 39 - 44.
8. Kaplan, pp. 82 - 88.
9. Lincoln Steffens, *The Letters of Lincoln Steffens*, ed. by Ella Winter and Granville Hicks (New York: Harcourt, Brace and Company, 1938), 1: 87 - 90. *New York Evening Post*, October 12, 1894, Steffens Collection.
10. *Autobiography*, 1: 179 - 86.
11. *Ibid.*, 1: 165, 179 - 96.
12. *Ibid.*, 1: 196.
13. *Ibid.*, 1: 241 - 42. "Murder—No Crime," 1898 (unpublished), Steffens Collection.
14. See Christopher Lasch, *The New Radicalism In America, 1889 - 1963: The Intellectual as a Social Type* (New York: Alfred A. Knopf, 1965), for a brilliant discussion of this subject.
15. *New York Evening Post*, March 16, 1897, Steffens Collection.
16. "Itzig's Wife," 1898, Steffens Collection. *New York Evening Post*, March 21, 1896, Steffens Collection.
17. *New York Commercial Advertiser*, October 5, 1898, Steffens Collection.
18. *New York Evening Post*, August 18, 1896, Steffens Collection.
19. *New York Evening Post*, September 17, 1896, Steffens Collection.
20. *Ibid.*
21. *Autobiography*, 1: 166; Kaplan, p. 82.

Chapter Two

1. *Letters*, 1: 98.
2. *Autobiography*, 1: 203 - 204; "Jacob A. Riis; Reporter, Reformer, American Citizen," *McClure's* 21 (August 1903): 419 - 25.

3. *Autobiography*, 1: 208 - 209; "Murder—No Crime."

4. *Sacramento Record Union*, June 1, 1894, Steffens Collection.

5. *Autobiography*, 1: 221 - 30, 286 - 87.

6. " 'Ashes?' A Dock Rat," 1900 (unpublished), Steffens Collection.

7. *Autobiography,*, 1: 197 - 200.

8. *Ibid.*, 1:231; *Letters*, 1: 90.

9. "Betrayed by His Horse," 1895 (unpublished), Steffens Collection.

10. *Autobiography*, 1: 223 - 24.

11. *Letters*, 1: 106, 197.

12. *Autobiography*, 1: 249.

13. *New York Evening Post*, October 18, 1896, Steffens Collection.

14. "Roosevelt," Steffens Collection. A form of this essay appeared as a series in the *New York Commercial Advertiser*, September 25, 1898; October 8, 1898; October 15, 1898.

15. *Ibid.*

16. *Autobiography*, 1: 257 - 58. *New York Commercial Advertiser*, May 7, 1898, Steffens Collection. *New York Evening Post*, Spring 1897, Steffens Collection.

17. *Sacramento Record Union*, April 11 - 13, 1895, Steffens Collection.

18. "As to Police Reform," 1902 (unpublished), Steffens Collection.

19. *Ibid.*

20. *Ibid.*

21. "The Man That Knows," 1900 (unpublished), Steffens Collection.

22. "The Banker's Love Story," 1902, Steffens Collection. This short story appeared in *Ainslee's*, October 1902.

23. *New York Evening Post*, March 21, 1895.

Chapter Three

1. *Autobiography*, 1: 311 - 19. Kaplan, pp. 82 - 88; Hutchin Hapgood, *A Victorian in the Modern World* (rpt. Seattle: University of Washington Press, 1972), pp. 138 - 40.

2. Kaplan, pp. 99 - 100; Ida Tarbell, *All In The Day's Work* (New York: Macmillan Company, 1939), pp. 200 - 201. Peter Lyon, *Success Story: The Life and Times of S. S. McClure* (New York: Charles Scribner's Sons, 1963), pp. 202 - 16, gives McClure most of the credit for the series.

3. "The Business of a Newspaper," *Scribner's Magazine* 22 (October 1897): 447 - 67.

4. Harold Wilson, *McClure's Magazine and the Muckrakers* (Princeton: Princeton University Press, 1970), pp. 191 - 97.

5. *The Shame of the Cities* (New York: Hill and Wang, 1957), p. 12.

6. *Ibid.*, p. 1.

7. *Ibid.*, p. 12.

8. *Ibid.*, pp. 2, 3, 7 - 9.

9. *Ibid.*, pp. 15, 18.

10. *Ibid.*, pp. 2, 18, 135 - 36.

11. *Ibid.*, pp. 3, 40.
12. *Ibid.*, pp. 20, 34, 87, 103, 108 - 109, 188 - 89.
13. *Ibid.*, pp. 4 - 5, 17, 20, 70.
14. *Ibid.*, pp. 20, 102 - 103.
15. *Ibid.*, pp. 10 - 11, 42. *Autobiography*, 1: 407.
16. *Shame of the Cities*, pp. 72 - 73, 44 - 46, 104 - 105.
17. *Ibid.*, pp. 74, 115 - 17.
18. *Autobiography*, 1: 434.
19. *Shame of the Cities*, pp. 20 - 23, 73, 106 - 107, 153 - 54.
20. *Ibid.*, pp. 43 - 49.
21. *Ibid.*, pp. 56 - 57, 116.
22. *Autobiography*, 1: 434.
23. *Shame of the Cities*, pp. 6, 21, 83 - 84.
24. *Ibid.*, p. 81.
25. *Ibid.*, pp. 42 - 43.
26. *Ibid.*, pp. 42, 134 - 37, 197.
27. *Ibid.*, p. 137.
28. *Ibid.*, pp. 198 - 201.
29. *Ibid.*, pp. 208 - 14.
30. *Ibid.*, pp. 19, 26 - 28, 32 - 33.
31. *Ibid.*, pp. 58 - 61, 26 - 27, 84 - 85.
32. *Ibid.*, pp. 58 - 59.
33. *Ibid.*, pp. 45, 60 - 64, 39, 90 - 96.
34. *Ibid.*, p. 69.
35. *Ibid.*, pp. 167 - 73.
36. *Ibid.*, pp. 165, 171 - 84.
37. *Ibid.*, pp. 10 - 11; Paul Conkin, *The New Deal* (New York: Thomas Y. Crowell, 1967), p. 12.
38. *Shame of the Cities*, pp. 214, 171.

Chapter Four

1. Samuel S. McClure, "Concerning Three Articles in this Number of McClure's, and a Coincidence That May Set Us Thinking," *McClure's* 20 (January 1903), p. 336.
2. Kaplan, pp. 110 - 18.
3. Wilson, pp. 200 - 14; *Letters*, 1: 165.
4. *Letters*, 1: 205, 168.
5. *Autobiography*, 1: 380 - 83, 400 - 402.
6. *Ibid.*, 2: 521 - 22.
7. *Ibid.*, 2: 523 - 24. See also Kaplan (pp. 128 - 29) and Lasch (p. 268), both superb discussions of this incident.
8. "The Honesty of Honest Tom," *McClure's* 45 (July 1915), p. 56.
9. *Autobiography*, 2: 524.
10. *Ibid.*, 1: 366 - 67, 416 - 19; 2: 482 - 86.
11. *Ibid.*, 2: 478 - 79. *The Struggle For Self-Government: Being an*

Attempt to Trace American Political Corruption to Its Source in Six States
(New York: McClure, Phillips and Company, 1906), pp. 183 - 98.

12. *The Struggle,* pp. v - xxiii.

13. *Ibid.,* pp. 3, 120 - 21, 151, 159 - 60.

14. *Autobiography,* 2: 454 - 63. *The Struggle,* pp. 81, 118 - 19.

15. Theodore Roosevelt, "The Man With the Muck-rake," *Outlook* 82
(April 21, 1906), 883 - 87. Kaplan, p. 142.

16. *Letters,* 1: 171.

17. *Autobiography,* 2: 535 - 36. Ray Stannard Baker, *American
Chronicle: The Autobiography of Ray Stannard Baker* (New York: Charles
Scribner's Sons, 1945), pp. 226 - 27.

18. *Boston Herald,* February 22, 1909, Steffens Collection; "Advice to
the First Voter," 1904 (unpublished), Steffens Collection; "Watch Your
Congressman," *Everybody's Magazine* 24 (May 1911), 708 - 10.

19. *The Shame of the Cities,* p. 98. "Roosevelt-Taft-LaFollette: On
What the Matter Is In America and What to Do About It," *Everybody's
Magazine* 18 (June 1908), 725 - 30.

20. "Hearst, The Man Of Mystery," *American Magazine* 48 (November
1906), 9 - 10, 22; *Autobiography,* 2: 541.

21. "Hearst," pp. 15, 20.

22. *Ibid.,* pp. 15, 18. *Autobiography,* 2: 542 - 43.

23. "Eugene V. Debs," *Everybody's Magazine* 19 (October 1908),
pp. 456, 61.

24. *Ibid., pp. 456 - 58.*

Chapter Five

1. *Letters,* 1: 202.

2. *Upbuilders* (New York: Doubleday, Page and Company, 1909),
p. vii.

3. *Ibid.,* pp. vii - ix, xv.

4. *Ibid.,* pp. x - xi, xv.

5. *Ibid.,* pp. 36, 66.

6. *Ibid.,* pp. 4 - 7, 129, xi.

7. *Ibid.,* pp. 47 - 52, 86.

8. *Ibid.,* pp. 152, 46, 148 - 49, 276.

9. *Ibid.,* pp. ix, 245 - 46, 278 - 81.

10. *Ibid.,* pp. 95 - 97, 101, 143, 148.

11. *Ibid.,* pp. 183, 192, 150, 224.

12. *Ibid.,* pp. 98 - 99, 224.

13. *Ibid.,* pp. 99 - 100.

14. Kaplan, pp. 166 - 70; *Letters,* 1: 218, 216. *Autobiography,* 2: 598 -
611.

15. Kaplan, pp. 171 - 72, 175; *Autobiography,* 2: 612 - 20.

16. "The Fruits of Good Government in New England," *Metropolitan*
39 (April 1914), 19, 62; "A Cure For Corruption," *Metropolitan* 39

(February 1914), 32; "Failure of Government by Good People," *Metropolitan* 39 (March 1914), 68 - 71; "A Way Out For Any City, State or Nation," *Metropolitan*, 40 (May 1914), 33, 52 - 54.

    17. "A Way Out," p. 33.

    18. "The Boss of All the Bosses," *Everybody's Magazine* 23 (September 1910), 292 - 94. This article is part 1 of a series entitled "It: An Exposition of the Sovereign Political Power of Organized Business."

    19. "The Politics of Business," *Everybody's Magazine* 23 (December 1910), 825.

    20. Horton, pp. 82 - 85; *Autobiography*, 2: 662.

    21. Kaplan, p. 189; *Autobiography*, 2: 663 - 64, 669.

    22. *Autobiography*, 2: 670 - 71, 677 - 83.

    23. *Ibid.*, 2: 788 - 89.

    24. *Ibid.*, 2: 627, 633.

    25. *Ibid.*, 2: 690. *Letters*, 2: 232 - 33.

    26. *Letters*, 1: 224.

    27. *Autobiography*, 2: 634 - 35, 653 - 54.

    28. *Ibid.*, 2: 654 - 55.

    29. *Ibid.*, 2: 655 - 56.

Chapter Six

    1. *Autobiography*, 2: 710.

    2. *Ibid.*, 2: 702.

    3. *Letters*, 1: 348.

    4. *The World of Lincoln Steffens*, ed. Ella Winter and Herbert Shapiro with introduction by Barrows Dunham (New York: Hill and Wang, American Century Series, 1962), p. 4, 78.

    5. Kaplan, pp. 211 - 12.

    6. *The World*, p. 4.

    7. "Smith of Guanajuato," 1922, Steffens Collection. Published under the title, "Those Lazy Mexicans," *Hearst's International* (May 1922).

    8. *The World*, pp. 4, 7, 12, 23.

    9. *Ibid.*, pp. 20, 22 - 23, 27.

    10. *Ibid.*, pp. 22, 28 - 29.

    11. *Ibid.*, pp. 28 - 29.

    12. *Ibid.*, p. 21.

    13. *Ibid.*, p. 5.

    14. *Ibid.*, pp. 5, 7, 23.

    15. *Ibid.*, p. 7.

    16. *Ibid.*, p. 6.

    17. Ibid., pp. 6 - 7. Norman Mailer, *The Armies Of The Night: History As a Novel, The Novel As History* New York: New American Library, A Signet Book, 1968), p. 174.

    18. *The World*, pp. 8 - 10.

    19. *Ibid.*, p. 10. *Autobiography*, 2: 716.

20. *Autobiography*, 2: 735 - 36. *The World*, p. 31.

21. *The World*, pp. 24, 14 - 15.

22. *Ibid.*, p. 24.

23. *Ibid.*, pp. 24 - 25.

24. *Ibid.*, pp. 24 - 26, 30.

25. *Ibid.*, p. 18. *Autobiography*, 2: 732, 743.

26. *The World*, p. 18.

27. *Ibid.*, pp. 24 - 26.

28. *Ibid.*, pp. 26, 31, 20.

Chapter Seven

1. *Autobiography*, 2: 813, 851.

2. Kaplan, pp. 216 - 25.

3. *Letters*, 1: 396 - 97, 414.

4. *Autobiography*, 2: 741. "What Free Russia Asks of Her Allies," *Everybody's Magazine* 37 (August 1917), 138 - 39.

5. *The World*, pp. 34, 39 - 40.

6. *Ibid.*, p. 39.

7. Steffens, "What Free Russia Asks," p. 132.

8. *Ibid.*, p. 133, *Upbuilders*, p. xi.

9. *Upbuilders*, p. xi; *The World*, p. 50; "What Free Russia Asks," pp. 132 - 35.

10. *The World*, p. 50, *Upbuilders*, pp. x - xi.

11. "The Rumor in Russia," *The Nation* 106 (December 1918), 766.

12. *The World*, pp. 45 - 47.

13. *Ibid.*

14. "The Rumor," p. 766; *The World*, pp. 47, 50.

15. "What Free Russia Asks," p. 133; *The World*, p. 48.

16. *The World*, pp. 44 - 45.

17. Henry May, *The End of American Innocence: A Study of the First Years of Our Own Time, 1912 - 1917* (Chicago: Quadrangle Books, 1964), pp. 3 - 107, 339 - 98.

18. Kaplan, pp. 244 - 51.

19. *Autobiography*, 2: 743, 780 - 86.

20. *Ibid.*, 2: 798 - 99.

21. *Ibid.*, 2: 813.

22. *The World*, pp. 55, 58; *Letters*, 2: 486.

23. *The World*, pp. 58 - 59.

24. *Ibid.*, p. 55; *Autobiography*, 2: 804 - 806.

25. *The World*, pp. 240 - 44, 258 - 59.

26. *Autobiography*, 2: 798.

27. *Ibid.*, 2: 815.

28. *Ibid.*, 2: 813 - 17.

29. *Letters*, 2: 525 - 27, 543 - 44, 622 - 25.

30. *The World*, pp. 75 - 76, 79.

31. *Ibid.*, pp. 70 - 73.
32. *Ibid.*, pp. 87 - 89.
33, *Ibid.*, p. 77.
34. *Ibid.*, pp. 103, 107 - 18, 139.
35. *Ibid.*, pp. 82 - 83, 85 - 86, 92.
36. *Ibid.*, pp. 102 - 106, 150.
37. *Ibid.*, p. 93.

Chapter Eight

1. Kaplan, pp. 272 - 80.
2. "Radiant Fatherhood: An Old Father's Confession of Superiority," in *Lincoln Steffens Speaking* (New York: Harcourt, Brace and Company, 1936), pp. 4, 13; *The Letters*, 2: 673.
3. *Speaking*, p. 19.
4. *The World*, pp. 235 - 37.
5. *Ibid.*, p. 195.
6. *Ibid.*, pp. 209 - 11.
7. *Speaking*, p. 19.
8. *Ibid.*, p. 16; *The World*, p. 196.
9. *The World*, pp. 196 - 97, 203.
10. *Speaking*, pp. 17, 91, 147, 153; *The World*, p. 201.
11. *Letters*, 2: 720 - 23, 737, 757.
12. Kaplan, pp. 291 - 97; *Letters*, 2: 869, 891 - 92.
13. *Letters*, 2: 719 - 20, 723 - 24.
14. For a brilliant discussion of American culture before World War I, see Henry May's *The End of American Innocence*.
15. *Autobiography*, 1: 357.
16. *Letters*, 2: 721.
17. *Ibid.*, 2: 722, 733 - 34, 760.
18. *Ibid.*, 2: 721 - 22; *Autobiography*, 2: 635.
19. See Christopher Lasch's *The New Radicalism* for a superb discussion of this question.
20. *Autobiography*, 1: 408, 2: 833.
21. *Ibid.*, 2: 821.
22. *Letters*, 2: 869.
23. *Autobiography*, 2: 749, 872.
24. *Ibid.*, 2: 873.
25. Kaplan, pp. 307 - 28.
26. *Speaking*, pp. 71 - 75, 297.
27. *Ibid.*, pp. 207 - 11, 225, 249 - 55, 260 - 62, 287.
28. *The World*, p. 215.

Selected Bibliography

PRIMARY SOURCES

The Lincoln Steffens Collection at Columbia University contains manuscripts (unpublished and published), letters, and scrapbooks of Steffens' newspaper and magazine articles. It is an invaluable source for Steffens' early writings. I found most of Steffens' magazine articles at the New York Public Library. It has one of the most extensive newspaper and periodical collections in the nation.

The Autobiography of Lincoln Steffens. 2 vols. New York: Harcourt, Brace and Company, 1931. Having fallen into undeserved obscurity after World War II, it has again taken its rightful place as an American classic.

The Letters of Lincoln Steffens. Ed. Ella Winter and Granville Hicks with memorandum by Carl Sandburg. 2 vols. New York: Harcourt, Brace and Company, 1938. An impressive collection of Steffens' correspondence from his student days in Europe to his death. The editors have not tried to hide any of Steffens' foibles and vanities and the result is a revealing portrait of the man and the writer. Consequently, it is often more informative about Steffens' private life and literary ambitions than *The Autobiography.*

Lincoln Steffens Speaking. New York: Harcourt, Brace and Company, 1936. A collection of vignettes, fables, essays, and articles written by Steffens during the last ten years of his life. They range in subject from politics to fatherhood.

The Shame of the Cities. New York: Hill and Wang, 1957. Steffens' first and best muckraking series collected into a book. The introduction is a superb example of the style, psychology, and politics of muckraking.

Struggle For Self-Government: Being an Attempt to Trace American Political Corruption to Its Source in Six States. New York: McClure, Phillips and Company, 1906. Another muckraking series collected into a book. It traces corruption from municipal governments into the states and, finally, to the United States Congress. It is the least interesting of his works.

Upbuilders. New York: Doubleday, Page and Company, 1909. The most underrated of Steffens' works. It is a thorough, often brilliant analysis of the relationship between the people and their leaders in a democracy.

The World of Lincoln Steffens. Ed. Ella Winter and Herbert Shapiro. New
York: Hill and Wang, 1962. A carefully selected collection of some of
Steffens' best postmuckraking writings. Well over half the volume is
devoted to his articles about the Mexican and Russian revolutions and
his defense of the Bolsheviks and communism. Of particular interest in
this regard is Steffens' *Moses In Red.* At the same time, there is a
representative sample of his articles concerning various other topics.

SECONDARY SOURCES

1.   Biographies and Autobiographies
BAKER, RAY STANNARD. *American Chronicle: The Autobiography of Ray
Stannard Baker.* New York: Charles Scribner's Sons, 1945. Baker, like
Steffens, focuses on his public life in his autobiography. A reluctant
muckraker, Baker provides an interesting view of the origins and the
course of muckraking. He portrays Steffens with affection, but is
critical of his later, radical politics.
CHESLAW, IRVING. "An Intellectual Biography of Lincoln Steffens." Ph.D.
dissertation, Columbia University, 1952. A thorough survey of
Steffens' social-political thought. The bibliography of Steffens'
writings is excellent.
HAPGOOD, HUTCHIN. *A Victorian in the Modern World.* Reprint. Seattle:
University of Washington Press, 1972. The author, who knew Steffens
for some forty years, has many interesting and delightful tales about
his old friend in his autobiography. There is, for example, an excellent
description of Steffens as city editor of the *Commercial Advertiser.*
HORTON, RUSSELL. *Lincoln Steffens.* New York: Twayne Publishers,
Twayne's World Leaders Series, 1974. For those unfamiliar with
Steffens, this is an effective introduction to his life and career.
KAPLAN, JUSTIN. *Lincoln Steffens: A Biography.* New York: Simon and
Schuster, 1974. A lucid, often brilliant biography. It is rich in detail
about his personal life and public career. As the only major biography
of Steffens, it is an invaluable source.
LYON, PETER. *Success Story: The Life and Times of S. S. McClure.* New
York: Charles Scribner's Sons, 1963. The definitive biography of the
founder and editor of *McClure's.* The book has an extensive discussion
of the working relationship between McClure and Steffens. The author
gives much credit for Steffens' success to his subject. In fact, he claims
that McClure initiated both the series on municipal corruption and the
one about state governments. Furthermore, he argues that McClure
provided Steffens with the thesis of *The Shame of the Cities.* This is
very different from Steffens' own account of muckraking in *The
Autobiography.*
WHITE, WILLIAM ALLEN. *The Autobiography of William Allen White.* New
York: MacMillan Company, 1946. This volume makes a splendid companion piece of Steffens' *Autobiography.* White and Steffens were

from similar backgrounds, both journalists, and they shared the same political views during much of the progressive movement. While White remained a typical American reformer, Steffens, of course, became a cosmopolitan radical. Taken by itself, White's *Autobiography* is a delightful tale of old fashioned midwestern society and politics.

WINTER, ELLA. *And Not to Yield; An Autobiography.* New York: Harcourt, Brace and World, 1963. This book has a loving, lovely portrayal of Steffens. It is one of the few glimpses of the private Steffens—husband, father, friend.

2. General Works and Anthologies

AARON, DANIEL. *Writers on the Left.* New York: Harcourt, Brace and World, 1961. A valuable work, which places Steffens within the modern Left literary tradition. It claims that *Moses In Red* and *The Autobiography* influenced many young writers and intellectuals to become Communists or Communist sympathizers.

CHALMERS, DAVID. *The Social and Political Ideas of The Muckrakers.* New York: The Citadel Press, 1964. A very brief survey of the thoughts of various leading muckrakers, including Steffens.

FILLER, LOUIS. *Crusaders For American Liberalism.* Yellow Springs, Ohio: The Antioch Press, 1964. This remains the standard work on muckraking. It is an exhaustive, sympathetic account of the muckrakers' efforts to expose and correct the worst evils of industrialization. Argues convincingly that economic pressure and reprisals from American business killed muckraking.

GRAHAM, OTIS. *An Encore for Reform: The Old Progressives and the New Deal.* New York: Oxford University Press, 1967. Examines how the progressives viewed the New Deal. Steffens was one of the few reformers who became more radical in those intervening years between Wilson and Roosevelt.

HARRISON, JOHN M., and STEIN, HARRY, eds. *Muckraking: Past, Present and Future.* University Park: Pennsylvania State University Press, 1973. This anthology of articles and essays discusses muckraking in all its various forms from its beginnings to the present. Jay Martin's "The Literature of Argument and the Arguments of Literature: The Aesthetics of Muckraking" is of particular interest to those dealing with the evolution of the muckraking style.

HOFSTADTER, RICHARD. *The Age of Reform: From Bryan to F.D.R.* New York: Vintage Books, 1955. Although subject to extensive revision, this remains a brilliant analysis of American Politics from populism to the New Deal. It recognizes the pivotal role of muckraking in the progressive movement. Muckraking is characterized as a striking combination of realism and Protestant moralism.

KAZIN, ALFRED. *On Native Grounds.* New York: Harcourt, Brace and Company, 1942. This seminal work on modern American literature sees

Steffens as the "evangelist" of the muckrakers. It underestimates his faith in democracy and misunderstands his early fascination with strong men.

LASCH, CHRISTOPHER. *The New Radicalism In America, 1889 - 1963: The Intellectual as a Social Type.* New York: Alfred A. Knopf, 1965. Useful to the student of Lincoln Steffens in two ways. First, it is a brilliant, if eclectic, study of the modern American intellectual. At the same time, it contains a perceptive essay about Steffens. Lasch believes that the intellectual must maintain a delicate balance between commitment and alienation. He finds in Steffens one of the few examples of this being successfully done. Finally, he is convinced that Steffens was always a radical.

MAY, HENRY. *The End of American Innocence: A Study of the First Years of Our Own Time, 1912 - 1917.* New York: Alfred A. Knopf, 1959. A superb analysis of the relationship between cultural perceptions and political thought in the years just prior to World War I. It traces the decline of nineteenth century culture as it began giving way to new ideas and innovative cultural forms. The book recognizes Steffens' role as a kind of midwife in the birth of this new cultural-political framework.

MOTT, FRANK LUTHER. *A History of American Magazines.* 5 vols. Cambridge: Belknap Press of Harvard University Press, 1968. A detailed survey of American magazines from the middle of the eighteenth century through the first decade of this century. While not very complimentary to muckraking, the work does show where muckraking fits into the history of American journalism.

WEINBERG, ARTHUR, and WEINBERG, LILA, eds. *The Muckrakers: The Era in Journalism That Moved America to Reform—The Most Significant Magazine Articles of 1902 - 1912.* New York: Simon and Schuster, 1961. This collection offers articles by such noted muckrakers as Ray Stannard Baker, Ida Tarbell, David Graham Phillips, and, of course, Steffens.

WILSON, HAROLD. *McClure's Magazine and the Muckrakers.* Princeton: Princeton University Press, 1970. This book places McClure and the muckrakers carefully and correctly within the American radical reform tradition. It brilliantly explains how muckraking was a combination of nineteenth century moral politics and twentieth century commercial and social realities. Finally, there is an involved and important analysis of Steffens' social-political philosophy.

3. Critical Essays

COCHRAN, BUD. "Lincoln Steffens and the Art of Autobiography." *College Composition and Communication* 14 (May 1965): 102 - 105. Analyzes *The Autobiography of Lincoln Steffens* as part of the literary tradition of autobiographical writing. While the author finds much to praise in

Steffens' *Autobiography,* he concludes that it is a failure as an autobiography. In his opinion, it is too much about society and politics and not enough about Steffens.

ROLLINS, ALRED. "The Heart of Lincoln Steffens." *South Atlantic Monthly* 59 (Spring 1960): 239 - 50. Portrays Steffens as a wrong-headed dogmatist. It is extremely critical of Steffens' radical critique of American politics and society. This article, written during the Cold War, helps explain Steffens' loss of popularity after World War II.

SCHULTZ, STANLEY. "The Morality of Politics: The Muckrakers' Vision of Democracy." *Journal of American History* 52 (1965): 527 - 47. Argues that the muckrakers' faith in democracy was based on a kind of secular moralism. Much of the article is devoted to Steffens' political philosophy, with particular attention being paid to his confidence in the American people.

STINSON, ROBERT. "Reconsideration: *The Shame of the Cities* by Lincoln Steffens." *The New Republic,* July 9, 1977, pp. 37 - 39. A thoughtful, provocative essay that analyzes the important contribution made by *The Shame of the Cities* to urban, progressive reform. It explains how Steffens manipulated the language and substance of the series to obtain a particular response from his readers. Finally, the essay provides a brief summation of modern criticisms of Steffens' findings and conclusions.

THELAN, DAVID. "Lincoln Steffens and the Muckrakers: A Review Essay." *Wisconsin Magazine of History,* Summer 1975, pp. 313 - 17. While praising Justin Kaplan's biography of Steffens, the review criticizes the author's judgment of muckraking and progressivism. This essay is one of the few that appreciates and understands the importance of *Upbuilders* as an explanation of the relationship between the people and their leaders in a democracy.

WILSON, EDMUND. "Lincoln Steffens and Upton Sinclair." *The New Republic* 72 (September 28, 1932): 173 - 75. An interesting comparision of the style and politics of Steffens and Sinclair by one of America's foremost critics.

Index

146